BOOKS

BOOK 1: THE KNIT STITCH

inspiration&instruction

the knitting experience

Sally Melville

The Knitting Experience Book I
PUBLISHED BY XRX BOOKS

PUBLISHER
Alexis Yiorgos Xenakis

EDITOR
Elaine Rowley

EDITORIAL ASSISTANT
Sue Nelson

KNITTING EDITOR
Gail McHugh

PROOFREADER
Holly Brunner

GRAPHIC DESIGNER
Bob Natz

PHOTOGRAPHER
Alexis Yiorgos Xenakis

FASHION EDITOR
Rick Mondragon

PHOTO STYLIST
Bev Nimon

ASSISTANT
Hannah Sorenson

DIRECTOR, PUBLISHING SERVICES
David Xenakis

PRODUCTION DIRECTOR
Dennis Pearson

BOOK PRODUCTION MANAGER
Natalie Sorenson

DIGITAL COLOR SPECIALIST
Jason Bittner

PRODUCTION
Everett Baker

TECHNICAL ILLUSTRATIONS
Jay Reeve
Carol Skallerud

SECOND PRINTING, 2003; FIRST PUBLISHED IN USA
IN 2002 BY XRX, INC.

ISBN 1-893762-13-0

Produced by XRX, Inc.
PO Box 1525
Sioux Falls, SD 57101-1525
605.338.2450

Contents

HAPPY DAY!

You've picked up this book. You are a person of incredible intelligence and creativity. You know that knitting is the coolest thing around, and it's time you learned how.

I don't want to slow you up for a moment. The steps on the next page are all you need to harness your unbridled enthusiasm and start knitting.

Needless to say, I hope you enjoy your experience and that it enriches your life. It certainly has that potential, as I have learned from the knitting I have done and the students I have taught.

Throughout this book I offer meditations on what knitting has taught me. If you never read these more reflective pieces, I'll never know. (Just like I never know if my family really listens to my ramblings while we sit and knit together. Don't tell anyone, but this is one of knitting's best features: you can sit and knit and be perfectly content, listening to someone who has a great need to talk.)

But if you do read them, know that these are the thoughts I would choose to share with you, if we were sitting and knitting together.

If you want a preview of these thoughts—and if you need any further encouragement to knit—read the one on page 7, How Knitting Can Change Your Life! But be aware that this is serious stuff, and it may alter your consciousness!

How to learn to knit

1 Look at the photos on the next few pages. These are some of the pieces in the book. Then look through the rest of the book for more. Find something you're excited about making. Check out its difficulty level. (In its pattern, under the word EXPERIENCE, you'll find bulleted notes referring to its difficulty level.) As a novice, you probably want to start with a 'beginner's first project.'

2 Before beginning the piece you want to make, spend time practicing The Basics (page 8). For this, don't go nuts buying supplies: you can borrow from a friend or—at most—buy just one ball of yarn and a circular needle. Your best choice would be an inexpensive, smooth, medium-weight yarn (which will show a suggested gauge of approximately 18 stitches/4" on the label) and a size 4 or 5mm/US 6 or 8 circular needle (20–24" long).

3 While learning, take time to read through the Choices chapter (page 130). It'll help you make the best decisions with respect to color, yarn, needles, and garment size. (If you choose to read this material later, that's fine. It can wait until you make something for which fit—and accurate measurement—matters.)

4 When you feel reasonably competent, take your pattern to the yarn shop for supplies.

5 If you need it, Ready to Start a Project (page 22) is a quick reference to guide you through your purchases and your pattern.

6 If you need it, the Oops! chapter (page 142) offers solutions to the most common mistakes.

7 If you need it, a mentor (a friend, the yarn shop owner) can help—because sometimes we need to see a live pair of hands working before we understand a maneuver.

46, 82

112, 104, 70

48, 107

107, 90

107

34

112

36, 70

66

70

112, 124

46, 104

46, 90

66

46, 121, 70

124

46, 70

HOW KNITTING CAN CHANGE YOUR LIFE!

Knitting is being called the 'new yoga.' It's a catchy phrase, and it speaks well of what we love about knitting: the beauty of its physical rhythm, the meditative state it induces, the community it fosters. But when asked why we knit, most will say something as inarticulate as, "It feels good!" What a concept! Doing something merely because it feels good!

If you think about it, this *is* a pretty powerful concept: doing something just because it feels good. In a world dedicated to productivity, it's pretty wonderful to give ourselves permission to do something just because it *feels* good.

And if this 'feel good' activity is something we can carry with us, wherever we go, that's pretty wonderful too! We'll never mind waiting. We won't struggle against time. We'll be more patient because we can always pick up our knitting and be happily engaged, wherever we are!

But, sitting and knitting and smiling and making the world a brighter place is not all we are doing. Whether we know it or not, we are enhancing our ability to live a creative life. (I warn you: here comes a potential *consciousness shift*.)

The human brain has two hemispheres, and they serve very different purposes. The *left brain* works to familiar patterns, rules, regulations, and in ways we have been taught to work. The *right brain* is the place where new ideas form, where entities that don't belong come together, where intuition rules, where time has no meaning.

We are a left-brain-dominant society. But as life offers problems for us to solve—where the old rules and regs don't apply—we need to get out of the dominant, full-of-rules left brain and into the more innovative, solution-advancing right brain. And we get into the right brain by engaging in activities that are
- physically repetitive,
- intellectually undemanding,
- visually stimulating.

Well! This explains the wonderful place to which my mind goes when I'm knitting. It also explains why I need time each day devoted to this kind of activity and away from the rigors of our left-brain-dominant culture.

Of course, there are all sorts of other activities that put us into the right brain: running, painting, potting, skiing, sewing, swimming, quilting, snow-boarding, sculpting, playing the piano, canoeing, crocheting, walking, weaving. Isn't it interesting that these activities are what we think of as things we do when we aren't working?

In fact, we might get some of our best thinking done when we're engaged in these activities. Imagine a world in which we are all expected to have hobbies—and to spend time at them regularly!

I don't remember much about learning to knit except that I was seven, and it was a pink piece of garter stitch. And I remember my mother looking over my shoulder and dealing with my impatience to reach the required four inches so I could start another piece.

It's thrilling to learn something new, at any age. But there are cautionary notes that come with the experience, and here they are.

- If you feel awkward, it does not necessarily mean that you are doing something wrong. It takes time to be comfortable, to find your method for holding needles and yarn, for achieving an even tension.

- While learning and perhaps a little tense, it's easy to knit too tightly. But the stitches may be so snugly wrapped around the one needle that it is difficult to drive the other needle through. This makes knitting more difficult than it needs to be. Have a glass of wine or a cup of tea, put on some great music, knit with friends, and try wrapping the yarn a little less tenaciously.

- One of the things I love about knitting is that it is not instant gratification. It's a wonderful experience to set a goal and learn the patience required to achieve it, anticipating the finish the entire time.

- Having said that, if you really hate the project you are working on, put it aside and try something else. You will learn that there are some yarns or needles or projects that just don't work for you.

- And having said all of the above, it's important to anticipate that you might find knitting *too* compelling. If you find yourself knitting without breaks for hours at a time, you run the risk of repetitive strain injury. Put an egg timer across the room, and set it to go off in 20 minutes. You are then forced to put down your knitting for a moment—to cross the room and set it to go off in another 20 minutes. (If you don't get up but continue to knit through the noise, get help! . . . and see a physiotherapist for preventative exercises.)

Basic skills

I am a right-handed person, so what do I know about living life left-handed? Not a lot. But what follows is after much discussion with left-handed knitters. I bow to their expertise, and here is what they said.

The world over, patterns are written for knit stitches to move from the left-hand needle to the right-hand needle. To knit left-handed has been understood to move stitches in the opposite direction of the more common way of working. This is also sometimes described as knitting 'backwards.'

The majority of the left-handed knitters with whom I spoke thought it a mistake to teach lefties to knit backwards. They did suggest that lefties might prefer the left-hand carry. In fact, in a very large guild with a 10% population of left-handed knitters, not one knit backwards . . . and 18 of 20 knit left-hand carry.

Having said that, we vary in the degree to which we are right- or left-handed. If you are one of those who is extremely left-handed, then you might find yourself, some day down the road, frustrated enough to choose to work 'backwards.' If this is you, don't let anything anyone else says dissuade you. Go ahead and work in any way that is comfortable. You will enjoy the process more, and the understanding you will bring to your knitting, as you re-interpret patterns, will make you a wonderfully intuitive knitter.

Right- and Left-handedness

Here are my thoughts on this central issue.
- Knitting is a two-handed activity: we simply choose to do more of the work with one hand or another, depending on our handedness.
- In this work, we hold a needle in each hand but we have a choice of hands with which to hold the yarn: right-hand carry or left-hand carry.
- In the earliest learning stages *only,* I suggest that right-handers use right-hand carry and left-handers use left-hand carry (as follows on pages 12–14).
- Once you become even slightly proficient, I suggest you try other methods (page 16). Again, knitting is a two-handed activity, so right-handers may switch to left-hand carry and vice versa. Try everything, then do what works.

Casting on at the beginning of a piece

At the beginning of your knitting, you need to have a base of stitches on a needle. This is called *casting on.*

The e-wrap cast-on

This easy, flexible cast-on is sometimes referred to as *the backwards loop cast-on.*

1 Holding needle and tail in left hand, put right index finger under yarn, pointing towards you.

2 Turn index finger to point away from you.

3 Insert tip of needle behind yarn on index finger.

Tail and Yarn

The *tail* is the thread at the beginning or end of a ball that is not knit but left hanging, to be sewn in later.
The *yarn* is the rest of the ball and what you'll knit with. For clarity, this is often called the *working yarn*.

If the piece for which you are casting on is to be seamed, leave the tail long enough to work the seam. (This will lessen the number of tails to be buried later.)

Here, the tail is on the left; the yarn is on the right.

The e-wrap cast-on will spiral around the needle even after a row is knit. Ignore this spiral if you are knitting back and forth in rows: it will disappear. Do not ignore it if you are knitting in rounds: it must be straightened (page 61).

To anchor your e-wrap cast-on, you may choose to start with a slip knot (page 18).

As you proceed with the e-wrap cast-on, the right degree of tension matters. You must pull the yarn fairly taut, but not so taut that the stitches are difficult to knit through. However, if you don't pull tightly enough, you will have large loops hanging from the bottom of your knitting. Do not despair; it can be tightened. See page 144.

Oops! As I knit the first row, one of my e-wrap cast-on stitches drops off the needle. What do I do now? See page 144.

4 Remove finger and draw yarn snug, forming a stitch. (This first cast-on stitch will not be very secure until you work the second.)

5 Repeat Steps 1–4 until required number of stitches is on left-hand needle. Try to maintain uniform spacing between cast-on stitches.

If you don't like the e-wrap cast-on, you may skip to the knitted cast-on (page 18), although it will be easier to master after you have learned the knit stitch. Alternatively, you may skip to the long-tail cast-on (page 58).

The knit stitch *k st*

A *stitch* is a loop of yarn on your knitting needle. As you knit, you will learn different kinds of stitches, but this book is dedicated to the knit stitch.

The *knit stitch* is formed by taking yarn around the right-hand needle and drawing it through a stitch on the left-hand needle, in the manner shown below.

To form the knit stitch, I suggest that right-handers use the right hand to carry the yarn (below) and left-handers use the left hand to carry the yarn (page 14). These methods are just the easiest way to get started. Don't worry if you feel awkward or slow. You'll soon have other choices.

Oops! As I knit the first row, one of my e-wrap cast-on stitches drops off the needle. What do I do now? See page 144.

THE RIGHT-HAND CARRY

1 With some number of stitches already cast on, and with yarn behind needles, put right-hand needle through first stitch on left-hand needle so right-hand needle sits behind left-hand needle.

2 Hold both needles with left hand, and hold yarn in right hand.

3 With right hand, wrap yarn around back of right-hand needle ...

6 ...then bring right-hand needle from behind left-hand needle to front of left-hand needle, without losing the loop on right-hand needle 'cause this is your new stitch!

7 Push right-hand needle off end of left-hand needle, so new stitch is on right-hand needle only.

KNIT STITCH • RIGHT-HAND CARRY

The right-hand carry and the left-hand carry are often given different names, based upon the geographical regions from which they originated. The right-hand carry is commonly known as the English or American method, while the left-hand carry is commonly known as the Continental or German method.

Knitters from all over the world use both, so I refer to the methods by what your hands are doing.

4 …then snug between two needles.

5 Draw right-hand needle down …

8 Repeat Steps 1–7 until all stitches are on right-hand needle.
If you started with the e-wrap cast-on, pull tail to tighten last stitch.

9 To begin next row, turn work …

10 …and transfer needle with stitches back into left hand.
For all following rows, repeat steps 1–9.

THE LEFT-HAND CARRY

1 With some number of stitches already cast on, and with yarn behind needles, put right-hand needle through first stitch on left-hand needle so right-hand needle sits behind left-hand needle.

2 Hold both needles with right hand, and hold yarn in left hand.

3 With left hand, take yarn in front of right-hand needle ...

4 ... then around to back of right-hand needle.

7 Push right-hand needle off end of left-hand needle, so new stitch is on right-hand needle only.

8 Repeat Steps 1–7 until all stitches are on right-hand needle. If you started with the e-wrap cast-on, pull tail to tighten last stitch.

9 To begin next row, turn work ...

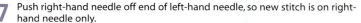

Garter stitch

Garter stitch is the name of the stitch pattern you are producing when you knit (as opposed to purl or slip or some other stitch manipulation) every stitch, every row.

It's very important that you remember that each garter ridge is two rows of knitting.

Every two rows produces one garter ridge, and these ridges are very easy to count. So, throughout this book, we refer to numbers of ridges rather than numbers of rows. But do remember that 1 ridge = 2 rows of knitting.

5 Draw right-hand needle down.

6 Bring right-hand needle from behind left-hand needle to front of left-hand needle, without losing the loop on right-hand needle 'cause this is your new stitch!

10 ...and transfer needle with stitches back into left hand.
For all following rows, repeat Steps 1–9.

This shows what garter stitch fabric looks like, plus how to recognize stitches and ridges. (The horizontal is a ridge, shown over 13 stitches; the vertical is a stitch, shown over 9 ridges.)

Oops! Something's wrong!

- **I put down my knitting to answer the phone, and now I don't know where I am.**
- **I dropped a stitch.**
- **Even worse, I dropped a stitch, and it unknit itself.**
- **I need to go back in this row.**
- **Gasp! I need to go back many rows.**
- **My knitting has a hole in it.**

Do not despair! This happens to all knitters. Wait'll you see how easy recovery, retrieval, and repair are! See pages 144–150.

For the record, I believe that with repetitive strain being such a concern for all of us who use our hands, it's best to master more than one method of holding the needles and carrying the yarn. You can then switch from one method to another to avoid the strain of repeating exactly the same movements.

When you switch from one method to another, at least at first, you might get a different look to each bit of knitting. But for the beginner garments in this book, these irregularities will not matter much.

Managing the yarn

Knitting can be slow and tedious (and possibly even cramp-inducing) if you continue as you were shown on the last four pages: 'fisting the yarn'—moving the entire hand—each time you work a stitch. Managing the yarn through your fingers is the first step to becoming more comfortable and efficient. What follows are the most usual choices.

Whichever of these choices you use, here's what threading the yarn through your fingers can accomplish:
- help you achieve even tension;
- help you minimize your movements.

FOR THE RIGHT-HAND CARRY

Put right-hand needle into first stitch on left-hand needle, as if to knit; this anchors your needle.
1 Put right pinkie, then right index finger, under yarn (above).

2 Put right index finger under yarn again, so there are two threads over index finger. Yarn on index finger sits at first knuckle, and just over an inch of yarn sits between the needle and the index finger.

Another method is to
1 wrap the yarn around the pinkie …

2 … before putting index finger under yarn.

FOR THE LEFT-HAND CARRY

Put right-hand needle into first stitch on left-hand needle, as if to knit; this anchors your needle.
1 Put left pinkie, then left index finger, under yarn (above).

2 Put left index finger under yarn again, so there are two threads over index finger. Yarn on index finger sits at first knuckle, and just over an inch of yarn sits between the needle and the index finger.

Another method is to
1 wrap the yarn around the pinkie …

2 … before putting index finger under yarn.

Holding the needles

The next step to becoming more comfortable, and more efficient, is to address how you hold your needles. What follows are the most usual choices.

THE OVER-THE-TOP HOLD *for right- or left-hand carry*
Every figure you've seen so far shows the over-the-top hold. It's kind of what we do naturally, regardless of which hand is carrying the yarn.

THE PENCIL HOLD *for right-hand carry only*
Even though we all hold pencils regularly, this hold can take some getting used to for knitting. However, it is my favorite method for holding my right-hand needle.

The over-the-top hold with the yarn in the right hand

The over-the-top hold with the yarn in the left hand

Hold left-hand needle in over-the-top hold. Hold right-hand needle in crook between index finger and thumb (rather like a pencil).

As knitting builds up onto right-hand needle, right thumb will have to move to under the fabric.

Right- and left-hand carries re-visited

Here's where you put it all together to find what works for you.

RIGHT-HAND CARRY
These photos show the pencil hold, but the steps will be the same for the over-the-top hold.

LEFT-HAND CARRY
Both right- and left-handers may use the left-hand carry, but handedness will be a factor, as shown below.

1 From starting position …

2 … slide the right-hand forward to take the yarn around the right needle. Open the space between your thumb and index finger to whatever degree feels comfortable.

Right-handers may move the right needle to wrap the yarn around the right needle. Arrow indicates the movement of the needle.

Left-handers may use the left index finger to wrap the yarn around the right needle. Arrow indicates the movement of the index finger.

The slip knot

Your cast-on may begin with this maneuver—a knot to sit on your left-hand needle and from which the casting-on of stitches begins. For the knitted cast-on, it is required.

1 Hold tail in left hand.

2 Wrap yarn around two or three fingers, forming a circle.

3 Insert tip of needle under back side of circle.

4 Draw yarn through circle, forming a loop on needle.

5 Remove fingers and pull both tail and yarn to tighten (above).

6 Put needle into left hand, and proceed to cast on stitches.

Oops! I started my cast-on with the slip knot, but it's ugly and I want to neaten it. What do I do now? See page 145.

The knitted cast-on

This cast-on provides a firmer edge than the e-wrap. Now that you know how to knit, it will be easily mastered.

1 Start with a slip knot on left-hand needle. Put right-hand needle into slip knot as if to knit.

2 Draw through a loop as if to knit.

3 Instead of sliding the new stitch off left-hand needle, make this loop a little larger than usual.

4 Put the loop back onto left-hand needle (above). Pull yarn taut.

5 Put right-hand needle into first stitch on left-hand needle. Repeat Steps 2–5 until required number of stitches is on left-hand needle.

If the piece for which you are casting on is to be seamed, leave a tail long enough to sew the seam. (This will lessen the number of tails to be buried later.)

Binding off at the end of a piece

At the end of your knitting, you need to close off the stitches. This is called *binding off* (sometimes referred to as *casting off*).

1 Work two stitches as usual. Insert left-hand needle into front of first stitch on right-hand needle.

2 Pass first stitch on right-hand needle over second stitch on right-hand needle (above). One stitch is bound off.

3 To continue, knit next stitch as usual, then repeat Steps 1–3 until only one stitch remains on right-hand needle.

4 Cut yarn to a minimum of 4". Make the last stitch bigger …

5 …then take it off the needle, draw the tail through this stitch, and pull to close.

Because of the nature of how it is formed, the bind-off can be the tightest 'row' of your knitting. It can even distort the shape of your knitting.

To prevent distortion, you might bind off with needles a size or two larger.

Alternatively, if your bind-off is too loose, it can be tightened. See page 149.

If the piece that you have just bound off is to be seamed, leave a tail long enough to sew the seam. (This will lessen the number of tails to be buried later.)

Care and feeding of your knits

In the patterns, directions will say *after blocking,* or *after pressing,* or *after washing.* It is important that you know how to do these, so as not to sabotage hours of knitting.

BLOCKING

This is a process to which we submit our knitting that
- sets the stitches,
- smooths out imperfections,
- shows what measurements we achieved,
- relaxes the fabric so it can be somewhat manipulated, if necessary, to achieve the measurements we really wanted,
- makes the pieces easier to seam.

Sounds great, we usually want to do it, and we usually want to do it before we sew the pieces together.

If the directions say *after blocking,* here's what you do.

1 Treat the piece as you would when you wash it.

2 Or, if you are in a hurry, give it a careful pressing on the wrong side of the fabric, using a steam iron set on wool with a wet cloth between the iron and the knitting.

Be very very cautious as you approach your knitting with an iron. Nearly every knitter I know has a horror story to tell— usually about too hot an iron producing a fabric too flattened and too shiny. Best to always have some moisture in the equation (in the fabric or the iron) and to never press the right side of your fabric, unless you are *sure* this is what you want to do. And *always* try it on your swatch before you try it on your garment.

PRESSING

Rarely do pieces need to be pressed. But if the directions say *after pressing,* here's what you do.

1 Use lots of steam (either in a steam iron or with a wet cloth between the iron and the knitting).

2 Use the lowest setting for steam (usually wool).

3 Press on both sides.

WASHING WOOL

We all know that wool shrinks, but we might not know that it shrinks with change in temperature plus water plus agitation. So we don't throw wet wool into the dryer. But it is just as damaging to wash it in warm water and then rinse it in cold. And, since wool is heavy when wet, we want to minimize handling.

Here is the best way to wash wool in a top-loading washing machine.

1 Fill tub with lukewarm water to cover garment.

2 Turn machine off.

3 Add 1 tablespoon Eucalan for each garment to be washed.

4 Add garment(s) and let soak for 45 minutes (if you need to remove dirt).

5 Do not rinse. (But do make sure the rinse cycle is set on *warm* so no cold water comes in during the spin. If your machine does not offer a warm rinse, turn off the water in-take.)

6 Turn machine to final spin (on delicate cycle, if you have one).

7 Remove garment after spinning.

Eucalan is available at most yarn shops. *Euca* is short for *eucalyptus oil*, which is a moth inhibitor. *Lan* is for *lanolin*, which restores natural oil to the wool and softens the garment. Both of these features are wonderful. But the best feature of this product is that it is not meant to be rinsed out, making it easy to wash a garment without much handling.

8 Lay flat, to desired shape and measurements (with a fan directed at the garment if you want to speed the drying process).

Here is the best way to wash wool by hand.

1 Follow Steps 1, 3, & 4, above, but in a sink.

2 Gently squeeze excess water from garment (with garment in pillow case for extra care).

3 Do not rinse.

4 Follow Step 8, above.

WASHING COTTON

Cotton garments can stretch, so here's how to wash a cotton garment and to bring it back to shape.

1 Wash on the gentle cycle in the machine but without using fabric softener.

2 Tumble in the dryer, checking frequently, until garment is desired size. If still damp, finish by drying flat.

3 If you over-use the dryer (and the garment dries too small) re-wash it, this time using fabric softener and being more careful with the dryer.

Brightly colored, non-mercerized cottons can fade over time, so while I prefer to wash, dry cleaning might be the best way to keep the colors true. White cotton can be bleached, although it will last longer if you neutralize the bleach—by adding white vinegar to the rinse (the same amount as the bleach used).

WASHING BLENDS OR SYNTHETICS

- If there is any wool in the fiber, treat it as wool.
- Acrylics (and other synthetics) are easy-care except that they can be easily burned—with a too-hot iron or in a too-hot dryer. If you burn a fabric that has any acrylic content, it will be permanently wrinkled.
- Save labels, with some yarn attached, for the fiber content and care instructions.

GENERAL CARE

- Don't hang knits; they're too apt to stretch and develop unsightly hanger bulges.
- Never store your garment dirty. Moths don't actually love wool; they love the dirt that resides there. A clean garment is likely to be overlooked. Does this mean you must wash your garment every time you wear it? No. Dirty means . . . well . . . stained, smelly, yucky. You'll know.
- Never store garments in direct sunlight. Some fibers will fade or discolor.

It is the most common of mistakes to not read the yarn label . . . and not determine the fiber content . . . and then to do something really foolish . . . like wash a garment with 15% wool in it as if it were 100% cotton (instead of the only 85% cotton as clearly reported on the label). The result may be the loss of a wonderful piece of hand-knitting!

I hesitate to report how often I have done this, but suffice to say that it is often enough that you would expect me to have finally learned this lesson.

The story about
this pattern

Notes
(to elaborate a point,
to coach you through
a process, to alert you
to an issue)

The vitals for
this pattern

The pattern instructions

Only the most obvious abbreviations are
used. The first time one is used in the
pattern, it will appear like this: knit (k).

The new skills you need are referenced
in the pattern. The first time one is used
in the pattern, it will appear like this:
cable cast-on, page 96.

For a quick reference to terms and
abbreviations, see the Glossary, page 152.

Fixing mistakes
Common mistakes are anticipated:
the remedies are in the Oops!
chapter, pages 142-150. As you
knit a pattern, check 'em out.

Additional skills
New skills are
found at the end of
each chapter

The drawing
a visual reference of
how this piece was
constructed plus all
its measurements

The yarn I used
and how much of it to
knit the size shown in
the photo

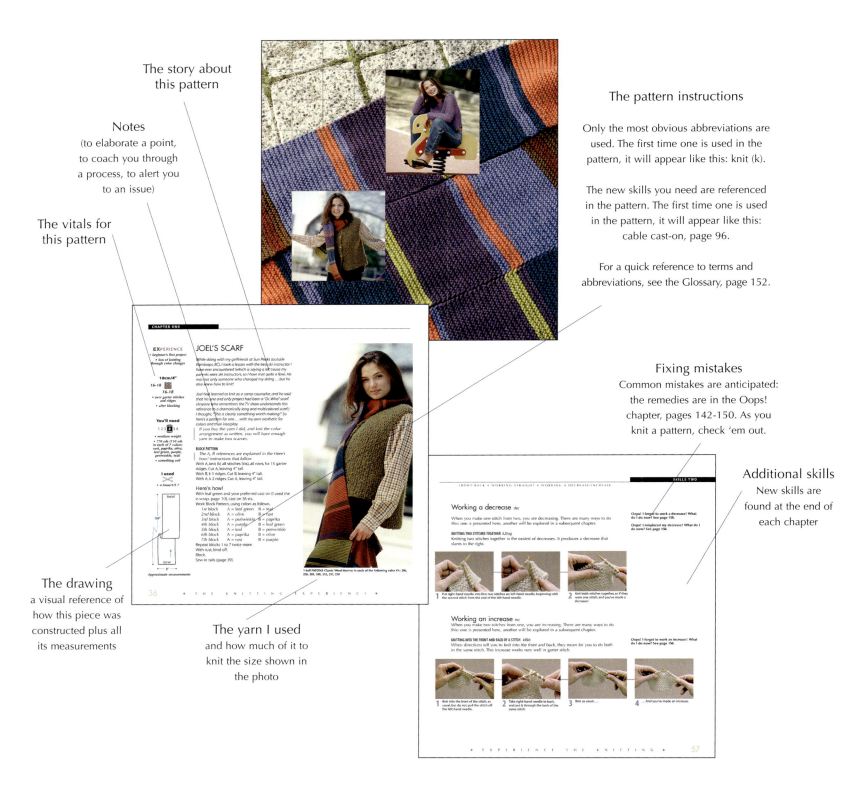

You're ready!

On these two pages is what you need to know to work through the patterns that follow.

The vitals column that accompanies every pattern is loaded with information, replacing a whole lot of words that can make knitting patterns look like no-fun text books. I think these icons are more knitter-friendly and more intuitive, and I know that they save page space. . . allowing me to include more patterns. But their most important function may be to make knitting a universal language.

EXPERIENCE
• *beginner's first project*

Difficulty rating The more bold letters, the more experienced you should be before you attempt the pattern.

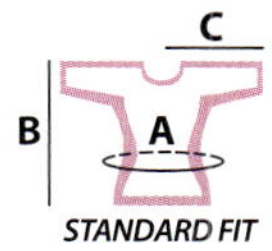

C
B | A
STANDARD FIT

Fit How closely the garment will fit your body, see page 139.

Woman's S (M, L)
A *40 (44, 48)"*
B *22"*
C *27"*

Sizes See page 138.
Measurements of the actual garment as they correspond to the A, B, C lines on the fit icon, see page 139.

10cm/4"

13 ▦ *GET GAUGE!*

13

• *over garter stitches and ridges*
• *after blocking*

Gauge The number of stitches you should have in 10cm or 4", see page 135.

Stitch pattern The kind of stitches you should use for your gauge swatch, and how it should be treated, see page 135.

You'll need

1 2 3 4 **5** 6

• *bulky weight*
• *450 (550, 750) yds*
• *something soft*

Yarn weight See page 133.

Amount of yarn See page 140.
Kind of yarn See page 132.

I used

✕

• *6mm/US 10*

Needles can be straight, circular, or double-pointed, see 134.
Needle size I used You may use another size based on your gauge swatch, see pages 135, 137–138.

THE KNITTING EXPERIENCE

FOR THE LOVE OF LEARNING

Here's what I know about learning.

1 Life is about learning. It makes good experiences thrilling and gives bad experiences meaning.

2 We can't love what we don't understand.

Here's how the first philosophy is manifested in this book.
- The projects are meant to support your learning and make it exciting.
- The Oops! chapter anticipates the mistakes you might make and shows how to fix them.

The second philosophy means that the book is organized so you will be taught
- *what* you need to know
- *when* you need to know it.

To teach this way means that you don't have to learn much before you can get started, that you don't have to feel overwhelmed with techniques, that you will understand what you are learning, that you will have confidence in what you are doing, that you will become an *intuitive* knitter.

To teach this way means that the book doesn't *look* like other instructional books. The methods for casting on or for increasing or for binding off aren't all lumped together. They appear *as you need them*.

To teach this way means that you don't learn *everything there is to know about knitting* in one book. This is not a complete knitting lexicon; it's a collection of the skills that I think you need to do a good job on these projects. Other knitters will show you different methods, and—by all means—learn whatever you can from whomever you can!

To teach this way also means that there is much more to come in *The Knitting Experience*.
- Book 2 covers the classic fabrics you can produce after you learn to purl.
- Book 3 covers the fabulous stuff you can make by changing colors in your knitting.
- Book 4 covers the delicious textures available in knitting.
- Book 5 covers the endless possibilities of what you can do when you learn to design your own stuff.

I'm working as fast as I can to produce these other books. In the meantime, if you choose to go there—to color and texture and design—faster than I can take you, I applaud you for your enthusiasm! Go there! There are lots of wonderful knitting books and magazines to lead you on this journey.

The first piece I knit for this chapter was Jen's Poncho, a large piece on thick yarn and big needles. It was for a young woman (my daughter), and she and her friends loved the result. So far, so good.

What else needed to go in this chapter? Surprise, surprise—beginner knitters kept saying that what they really wanted to knit was a scarf. So, it was my challenge to come up with different ways to do something as simple as a scarf.

The Three-scarf Ruana came last. Kind of a hybrid of the other pieces, it was my attempt to design something more complex than the scarf and more sophisticated than the poncho.

While the pieces of this chapter are easy—simple squares or rectangles made into garments—there is, except for the Minimum Scarf, a lot of fabric to knit, and certainly not on thick yarn and big needles. Is this something beginners will be willing to do?

If you are not willing to commit to a large project, go to the next chapter. But first consider this. To learn to knit, you need to practice . . . on something with enough knitting so your skills can develop. And it's sometimes easier on your hands if this is not done with thick yarn and big needles. Hence the projects of this chapter: three projects on smaller needles and finer yarn, one on larger needles and thicker yarn, but all requiring lots of knitting.

Chapter One

The Patterns

Additional Skills

MAXIMUM SCARF

10cm/4"

15-17

18-20
- over garter stitches and ridges
- after blocking

You'll need

1 2 3 **4** 5 6

- medium weight
- 825 yds
- something soft

I used

- 5mm/US 8

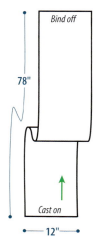

Approximate measurements

I do understand the desire to knit a scarf. It's kind of a traditional first project, often given away to a loved one. Plus its gauge doesn't really matter: do we really care what size it is? Also, the knitting is easy and endlessly repetitive with lots of yardage upon which to practice. Finally, if there are irregularities, who's to see them buried in the folds?

Here's how!

With your preferred cast-on (I used the e-wrap, page 10), cast on 60 stitches (sts).

> *There is no need to make the scarf to the size suggested. You may make a smaller piece by casting on fewer stitches and working fewer rows. At a gauge of approximately 5 stitches per inch, multiply 5 by the number of inches wide you want the piece, cast on that number of stitches, then knit to desired length.*

Knit all sts, all rows, to desired length (or until no less than 48" of yarn remains at the beginning of a row).

Bind off.

Block piece.

Sew in tails (page 39).

5 skeins GARNSTUDIO Karisma Angora-Tweed in color #10

3 balls MUENCH Touch Me in color #3620

MINIMUM SCARF

While the first scarf is an enveloping muffler, this is meant to be more of a dress-up version, in a truly luscious yarn and in a color you adore.

The model piece is knit in garter stitch, but it looks like something different. That's because I used a to-die-for yarn and then treated it; see notes that follow. This treatment is essential to this particular yarn, and changes the fabric.

Here's how!

With your preferred cast-on (I used the e-wrap, page 10), cast on 32 stitches (sts).
Knit all sts, all rows, to desired length (or until no less than 24" of yarn remains at the beginning of a row).
Bind off.
Sew in tails (page 39).

> *Special note for Touch Me:*
> *As you knit, occasional loops (called worms) may appear . . . from nowhere and when you weren't looking. Don't fret! They disappear when you wash the piece. Despite what the yarn label says, wash and rinse in warm water in the washing machine. It will come out of the washer small and hard. Dry it in a warm dryer, and it will soften to something extraordinarily beautiful, a little narrower than what you knit. The tails may come loose after washing; just sew them back in.*

EXPERIENCE
- *beginner's first project*

10cm/4"

15-17

15-17
- *over garter stitches and ridges*

You'll need

1 2 3 **4** 5 6

- *medium weight*
- *180 yds*
- *something luscious*

I used

- *5mm/US 8*

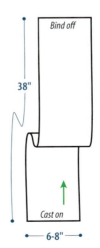

Bind off

38"

Cast on

6-8"

Approximate measurements

HAVE FUN! SCARF

The fun begins with your trip to the yarn shop ... where you get to buy four skeins of anything that appeals to you! You might start with the funnest yarn you can find, in a color you like, then add three more yarns that coordinate.

This scarf is knit by casting on the stitches for the length and then knitting—one row in each yarn—to the desired height. This is sometimes referred to as knitting lengthwise.

What about all those tails, as you change yarn every row? Leave them long, don't sew them in, and they become the fringe!

EXPERIENCE
- *beginner's first project*

10cm/4"

11-13

11-13

- *over garter stitches and ridges*
- *after pressing*

You'll need

1 2 3 **4-5** 6

- *medium or bulky weight*
- *500-600 yds total*
- *4 or more novelty yarns*

I used

- *5.5mm/US 9*

Overhand knot

Here's how!

Leave 8" tail (for fringe). With yarn of most yardage and your preferred cast-on (I used the e-wrap, page 10), cast on 175 stitches (sts). Leaving 8" tail (for fringe), cut yarn.

Leaving 8" tail, tie an overhand knot with strand of next yarn and tail from last row, and knit all sts. Leaving 8" tail at end of row, cut yarn. Repeat from.

> *It's important to distribute your yarns so you don't run out of one too early. If you have a yarn with less yardage, skip its use occasionally. If you have a yarn with more yardage, repeat its use more frequently.*

When the scarf is desired height or when you run out of a yarn, bind off loosely.

Trim tails to suit.

Press on wool setting, on both sides, with lots of steam.

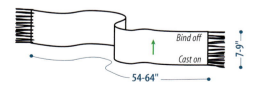

Bind off

Cast on

7-9"

54-64"

Approximate measurements

1 skein each of the following yarns: PRISM Tubino in color Orient Express and Panther in color Cabernet; GREAT ADIRONDACK YARN CO. Ballerina in color Cancun and Funky in color Fire

Child's 4–6: 5 balls STYLECRAFT Braemar in color #3286

JEN'S PONCHO

This poncho has quite a history!

I knit the first one as a birthday present for my daughter, Caddy. Her best friend, Jen, wanted to learn to knit, but only on a small project, so she knit the child's version. It was done in a matter of days, and she did a fabulous job.

Jen then decided to make a larger one for herself. She had knit the child's size from 5 balls of yarn but, after buying the yarn for the adult size, she called a day later in a panic: "I can't knit with this stuff! It's a mess!" After a bit more information, it became apparent that she had tried to knit right from the skein, without first winding it into a ball.

As someone who has been knitting for 45 years, this was a significant reminder that—for this book—I had to put my head in a different place, to not take anything for granted. Right! Yarn comes in both balls and skeins, with the latter requiring winding into the shape of the former.

We rescued Jen's yarn, and she knit her poncho. (It's the adult's medium version shown on page 33.)

The end of this story is that, many months later, Caddy finally decided to learn to knit — a happy day for me! She knit the off-white version of this poncho, beautifully and with very little help. One of the first times she wore it, someone admired it, and she got to say—ever-so-proudly— "I made it myself." What a wonderful moment for a new knitter!

EXPERIENCE
- *beginner's first project*
- *lots of knitting*
- *minimal finishing*

It'll fit

Child's 4–6 (8–10, Adult's short, medium, long)

10cm/4"

9 GET CLOSE

9

- *over garter stitches and ridges*
- *before blocking*
  - *child's– soft wool blend*
  - *adult's– wool or wool blend*

You'll need

1 2 3 4 5 **6**

- *super bulky weight*
- *420 (500, 530, 590, 720) yds*

I used

- *8mm/US 11, 60cm/24"*

- *8mm/US L*

JEN'S PONCHO

Here's how!

RECTANGLE

With your preferred cast-on (I used the e-wrap, page 10), cast on 32 (37, 43, 48, 54) stitches (sts).

Knit (k) all sts, all rows, to 48 (53, 61, 66, 72) garter ridges.

This is a large number of ridges to knit. Hang something—a piece of yarn, a paper clip—every 20 ridges, so you don't have to continuously re-count.

When you come close to the end of a ball (page 38), you could start the new ball of yarn at the beginning of the next row. Some tails will be woven into seam allowances, but others can be taken into fringe. Be sure to leave these tails the length you think you might want fringe.

Bind off.

Now make a second piece, exactly as the first.

You could block the pieces, but they will soften best, and go to their final measurements, if you wash them and lay them flat to dry.

If the pieces achieve the measurements you expected, great! If not, don't worry. The garment will 'fit,' even if the measurements you produce are not what you intended. (My daughter's off-white was to be a Medium and was a Short instead. No problem! She just made the fringe a little longer.)

FINISHING

Determine right side (RS) of pieces, and do what follows with RS facing.

Place rectangular pieces perpendicular to each other so that the bound-off edge of one piece aligns with the ridged edge of the other; 7 (7, 8, 8, 8)", 16 (16, 18, 18, 18) ridges, should remain clear at the top.

See drawing to help visualize this.

Sew 1 bound-off st to each garter ridge (page 42), where shown by jagged line on the drawing.

Fold pieces to align other bound-off edge with other ridged edge, and sew second seam.

There is now a V-neck opening at the top! Isn't that cool?!

If there are any tails along the seam lines, sew to wrong side (WS).

NECK EDGING

Try your poncho on: if you like how it sits around the neck, then wear it as is. If you wish the neck were a little tighter or neater, apply the following edging.

With RS facing and beginning at point of V, pick up 1 st for every ridge (page 41) around entire neck opening— 32–34 sts picked up for child's, 36–38 sts picked up for adult's.

Bind-off row Introduce yarn and working loosely, bind off picked-up sts.

Sew in tails to WS (page 39).

FRINGE

Decide how long you want the fringe. For 3" fringe, find a book with a circumference of approx 8"; for a 5" fringe, find a book with a circumference of approximately 12". (Book circumference = [length of fringe x 2]+2".)

Wrap yarn around book and cut, to make pieces of uniform length.

Attach 2 fringe pieces, at every 2nd st and every 2nd ridge, around entire lower edge of poncho as follows: holding 2 fringe pieces, fold in half; insert crochet hook, from WS to RS, through edge of garment st or ridge; draw fold of fringe through to form a loop; pull cut ends of fringe through this loop.

Include yarn tails in fringe as you encounter them.

Trim fringe to suit.

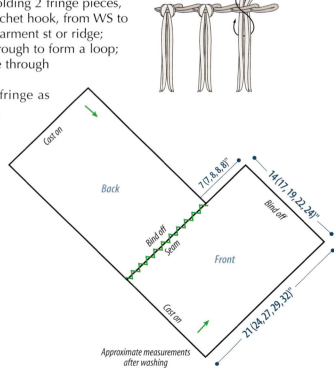

Attach fringe

Cast on

Back

7(7, 8, 8, 8)"

14(17, 19, 22, 24)"

Bind off

Bind off

Seam

Front

21(24, 27, 29, 32)"

Cast on

Approximate measurements after washing

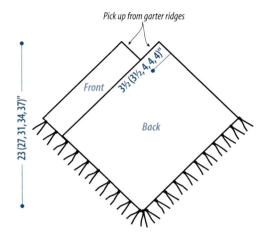

Pick up from garter ridges

Front

Back

3½ (3½, 4, 4, 4)"

23 (27, 31, 34, 37)"

Above, Adult's S: 8 skeins ISTEX Bulky Lopi in color #0051; shown with Have fun! Scarf: 1 skein each PRISM Tubino in color Jet, Panther in color Embers, and Lazer in colors Embers and Mink
Left, Adult's M: 9 skeins ISTEX Bulky Lopi in color #9417

EXPERIENCE

- *beginner's first project*
- *lots of knitting*
- *minimal finishing*

10cm/4"

17 GET CLOSE

19

- *over garter stitches and ridges*
- *after blocking*

You'll need

1 2 3 **4** 5 6

- *medium weight*
- *1650 yds*
- *soft wool or wool blend*

I used

- *4.5mm/US 7*

10 skeins GARNSTUDIO Karisma Angora-Tweed in color #01

THREE-SCARF RUANA

A ruana is a one-size-fits-all, classic South American garment. It is usually made from two rectangles; here, a third rectangle is attached at the neck to add interest, sophistication, and warmth.

Yes, there is lots of knitting ... and in a not-terribly-thick yarn. But you may find, as you knit more and more, that your hands prefer to knit finer rather than thicker yarns. And, if you choose to make this garment, your knitting skills will be well-developed upon its completion.

Here's how!

HALF GARMENT

FRONT

With your preferred cast-on (I used the e-wrap, page 10), cast on 60 stitches (sts).
Knit (k) all sts, all rows, to 35".

NECK OPENING

At beginning of next row, k 38 sts, then put next 22 sts onto a holder.
Turn (page 40) and e-wrap cast on 22 sts onto left-hand needle—60 sts on needle.

BACK

K all sts, all rows, until the back is the same length as the front.
Bind off.

Now make a second piece, exactly as the first.
Don't worry about which is the right or wrong side, or the right or left front. That's sorted out later.

COLLAR

1 Designate one piece as the right (R). Turn left (L) piece over so it is a mirror image of the R.

2 Sew pieces together (ridges to ridges, page 42) along center back, working from collar downward, for approximately 14".

3 Beginning at R front neck opening, k 22 sts from holder. Pick up and k 1 st at corner (page 40).
Turn corner, then pick up and k 22 sts along cast-on edge of R back neck.
Working continuously, pick up and k 22 sts along cast-on edge of L back neck.

Pick up and k 1 st at corner.
Turn corner, then k 22 sts from holder at L Front neck—90 sts on needle.

4 Turn, and cast on 60 sts onto left-hand needle.
These 60 sts becomes the L front 'scarf.'
K all 150 sts.

5 Turn work, and cast on 60 sts onto left-hand needle.
These 60 sts becomes the R front 'scarf'.
K all 210 sts, all rows, to 6".
Bind off.
Press lightly with steam.

FINISHING

Try garment on.
You will see 'wings' at the shoulderline. Don't be alarmed; we're going to remove them!
On one shoulder, pinch material and fold, forming dart. Pin down. (Dart will be approximately 4" long, with 3" of fabric taken out at the edge.)
Take garment off, and pin other shoulder to match. (Try it on again to make sure you like what you have done and to make any adjustments.)
With yarn of garment, sew along pins then lightly stitch darts to wrong side (WS) of ruana.
Press lightly.
Sew in tails to WS (page 39).
Sew brightly colored thread (or a personal label!) to inside of back neck. This will designate the inside so you know which way to wear the garment.

5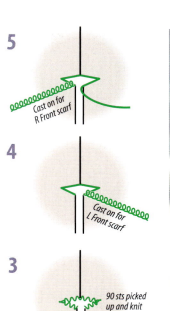
Cast on for R Front scarf

4
Cast on for L Front scarf

3
90 sts picked up and knit

2
R Back | Seam | L Back
R Front | L Front
Sts on holders

1
Bind off | Bind off
R Back | L Back
Cast on sts for back neck
Sts on holder for front neck
R Front | L Front
Cast on | Cast on

6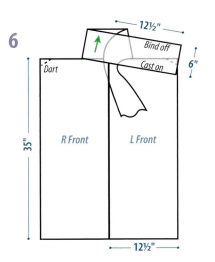
12½"
Bind off
Dart
Cast on
6"
35"
R Front | L Front
12½"

EXPERIENCE
• beginner's first project
• lots of knitting through color changes

10cm/4"

16-18

16-18

• over garter stitches and ridges
• after blocking

You'll need

1 2 3 **4** 5 6

• medium weight
• 770 yds (110 yds in each of 7 colors: rust, paprika, olive, leaf green, purple, periwinkle, teal)
• something soft

I used

• 4.5mm/US 7

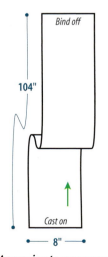

Bind off

104"

Cast on

8"

Approximate measurements

JOEL'S SCARF

While skiing with my girlfriends at Sun Peaks (outside Kamloops, BC), I took a lesson with the best ski instructor I have ever encountered (which is saying a lot 'cause my parents were ski instructors, so I have met quite a few). He was not only someone who changed my skiing ... but he also knew how to knit!

Joel had learned to knit as a camp counselor, and he said that his one and only project had been a "Dr. Who" scarf. (Anyone who remembers the TV show understands this reference to a dramatically long and multicolored scarf.) I thought, "This is clearly something worth making!" So here's a pattern for one ... with my own aesthetic for colors and their interplay.

> *If you buy the yarn I did, and knit the color arrangement as written, you will have enough yarn to make two scarves.*

BLOCK PATTERN

> *The A, B references are explained in the Here's how! instructions that follow.*

With A, knit (k) all stitches (sts), all rows, for 15 garter ridges. Cut A, leaving 4" tail.
With B, k 3 ridges. Cut B, leaving 4" tail.
With A, k 2 ridges. Cut A, leaving 4" tail.

Here's how!

With leaf green and your preferred cast-on (I used the e-wrap, page 10), cast on 36 sts.

> *To make a skinny scarf, cast on 24 stitches, and work as directed. You'll need a little less yarn.*

Work Block Pattern, using colors as follows.

1st block	A = leaf green	B = teal
2nd block	A = olive	B = rust
3rd block	A = periwinkle	B = paprika
4th block	A = purple	B = leaf green
5th block	A = teal	B = periwinkle
6th block	A = paprika	B = olive
7th block	A = rust	B = purple

Repeat blocks 1 to 7 twice more.
With rust, bind off.
Block.
Sew in tails (page 39).

1 ball PATONS Classic Wool Merino in each of the following color #'s: 206, 238, 205, 240, 212, 213, 218

What to do at the end of a ball

If your project uses more than one ball of yarn, you need to deal with moving from the end of one ball to the beginning of another. Or you may run into a knot in your yarn and wish to remove it, so you are then faced with the same situation—a break in your yarn.

JOINING YARN MID-ROW
Here is the easiest way to join new yarn in the middle of a row.

When you have a 5" tail of the old ball, add the new ball as follows.

1 Leaving a 4" tail of the new ball on the wrong side of work (above), knit one stitch with both the new yarn and the old tail together.

2 You will have produced a 'doubled' stitch (above). Drop the old tail on the wrong side of work, and continue only with the new yarn.

3 When you encounter this 'doubled' stitch on the next row, knit it as one stitch (above). Sew in both tails when finished.

JOINING YARN ONLY AT ENDS OF ROWS
Sometimes you don't want to join yarn mid-row. You want to end one ball and begin another at the end of a row, leaving tails to be sewn in later. But this begs the question, 'How do you know if you have enough yarn to finish a row?'

It takes approximately three times the width of the piece to work one row, plus an allowance for the length of tail. It takes approximately four times the width of the piece to work the bind-off row.

Right side and wrong side *RS WS*

In knitting, as in most things, the *right side* is the public side, the *wrong side* is the non-public side. Most knitting has an obvious right or wrong side: the seam allowances usually designate the wrong side. But if knitting looks the same on both sides, look at the cast-on or bind-off to see which side you prefer as the right side.

If you need to know right or wrong side while knitting, I recommend hanging a marker (something as simple as a paper clip) on the wrong side of your knitting.

Sewing in tails in garter stitch

1 Thread tail into a tapestry needle, and—if it isn't already there—bring it to the wrong side of the work.

2 Sew in and out of garter bumps, for 2".

3 Turn …

4 …then work in the opposite direction, for 1".

5 Trim tails to no less than ½".

For clarity, the tails are shown in contrasting-color yarn.

Here are two sewn-in tails, both working away from a mid-row join.

On the right side, the tails are not visible.

In Chapter 2, you will learn about stockinette stitch. And even though stockinette and garter look different, sew in your stockinette stitch tails just as shown here—along a row of bumps. Even if the bumpy side is the right side of your stockinette stitch garment, the sewn-in tails won't be visible. But do bring the tail ends to the wrong side of the piece before clipping to ½".

Knitting in tails

In this method, you don't have to go back later and sew in the tails. However, not all yarns are suited to this method: the doubling of yarn may be visible.

When you have a 5" tail of the old ball, add the new ball as follows.

1 Leave a 1" tail of the new ball on the wrong side …

2 … then knit 4–6 stitches with the new yarn and the old tail held together (above).
Drop the old tail on the wrong side of work, and continue with only the new yarn. Trim tails to no less than ½".

3 On the next row, you will have stitches with doubled yarn. Work them as single stitches.

Knit-in tails, right side facing

Turning

When knitting directions say to *turn,* they mean to turn the knitting around to the opposite side, even if you are in the middle of the row.

Right and left *R L*

When talking about hands, it's easy enough to know which is right or left. But what about garment pieces? What does a pattern mean when it speaks of the *Right Front?* This designation refers to the piece as you will wear it. The right front will sit on the right side of the body, the left on the left side of the body.

Picking up

PICKING UP AND KNITTING ALONG A CAST-ON EDGE

Look at the pattern to see how many stitches were cast on. Now look at your work to recognize the spaces that represent these cast-on stitches and to see where you will pick up the required number of stitches.

1 Put right-hand needle into the space that represents the first cast-on stitch. (If right-hand needle is under two threads, the result will be less holey and more secure.)

2 Wrap working yarn around right-hand needle and draw through, to form a stitch.

3 Put right-hand needle into the space that represents the next cast-on stitch (above). Repeat Steps 2–3.

Five stitches, picked up and knit

PICKING UP FROM GARTER RIDGES

1 With right side facing, put left-hand needle, from left to right, through the same part of each garter ridge, close to the edge. This shows four ridges picked up, ready to pick up a fifth.

2 If the pattern tells you to knit them, use working yarn and do so as usual. This shows five stitches knit and some picked-up garter ridges waiting to be knit.

PICKING UP AND KNITTING BETWEEN GARTER RIDGES

To pick up and knit between garter ridges, notice the edge between the stitch you have just knit and the next stitch to be knit off left-hand needle (above).

1 Insert right-hand needle into this edge (as shown by arrow), and draw working yarn through to form a new stitch.

A new stitch, picked up in the space between garter ridges

PICKING UP/PICKING UP AND KNITTING

These two terms mean different things. They both have you putting stitches onto a needle but in different ways.

- To *pick up,* use your left-hand needle and no yarn and move from left to right. When done, no new row has been knit. (See Step 1 in Picking up from garter ridges.)
- To *pick up and knit,* use your right-hand needle and working yarn and move from right to left. When done, one new row has been knit. (See step 2 of Picking up and knitting along a cast-on edge.)

There are many wonderful people devoting lots of time to the standardization of knitting terms. Until this job is done, there are times when you simply will not be given enough information, but you will be expected to know what to do and how to do it.

The distinction between *picking up* and *picking up and knitting* is made to help you sort this out . . . to help you become a more intuitive knitter.

Seaming in garter stitch

There are three types of seams to make in garter stitch: where ridges match up with ridges, where stitches match up with stitches, and where stitches match up with ridges.

RIDGES TO RIDGES

Whew! Who needs to know three kinds of seaming? Well, you need to know how to seam ridges to ridges for the back seam of the Three-scarf Ruana. And you need to know how to seam stitches to ridges for Jen's Poncho. You will not need to know how to seam stitches to stitches until Chapter 3.

Do all of this with right side facing.
1 Take tapestry needle under one garter ridge, close to the edge of the piece.

2 Go across to opposite piece. Take tapestry needle under matching ridge.

3 Go back to first piece. Take tapestry needle under next ridge (above). Repeat Steps 2–3.

For clarity, seaming is shown with contrasting-color yarn.

STITCHES TO RIDGES

Sometimes the yarn of the garment is appropriate for seaming, and sometimes it's not. It's preferable to use the yarn of the garment, but if it catches or tears, substitute a smooth yarn in an appropriate color.

Do all of this with right side facing.
1 Take tapestry needle under first garter ridge, close to the edge of the piece.

2 Go across to other piece. Take tapestry needle under first stitch, above bind-off edge.

3 Go back to first piece. Take tapestry needle under next garter ridge.

Five ridges sewn, before pulling yarn taut

Five ridges sewn, after pulling yarn taut

To make these seams look neat, be consistent. When you find the part of the garter ridge that you want to use for the seam, be sure to choose the corresponding part of all garter ridges for the duration of the seam. Attention to these details really matters.

As you seam, pull your sewing yarn taut— just to resistance and not so you pucker your seam—every inch or so.

4 Go across to opposite piece. Take tapestry needle into space you came out of and then under next stitch (above).
Repeat Steps 3–4.

Five ridges and five stitches sewn, before pulling yarn taut

Five ridges and stitches sewn, after pulling yarn taut, with the bind-off edge into seam allowance

Beginning and ending with

When a pattern says *beginning with,* it means that what follows is what you do next. For example, *beginning with a right-side row* means your next row is a right-side row.

When a pattern says *ending with,* it means that what follows is what you have just finished. For example, *ending with a wrong-side row* means you have just finished a wrong-side row.

The projects in this chapter differ from the previous in two significant ways: none of them require a whole lot of knitting, and all of them require some sort of shaping.

The first projects that I actually knit for this chapter—the Knit-flat hat and mitts—were the most difficult. I have thought about why I do this (start a chapter by knitting its most difficult piece), and I think it's to establish a bottom line: here is the level of difficulty beyond which this chapter should not go, so work back from here. The challenge then was to see how easy the pieces could become.

Some of these projects are incredibly easy: the Shape it! scarf is one of the easiest I have ever designed. But it's also an amazing piece that even experienced knitters will want to make and own.

This chapter contains some of my favorite pick-up-and-take-anywhere knitting. It's stuff for which I am constantly buying yarn so I can be knitting on a piece—for myself or for someone else—wherever I go. And if you work through this chapter, I expect you'll find favorites of your own.

Chapter Two

The Patterns

Additional Skills

3 balls LANO GATTO Batik in color #2601

SHAPE IT! SCARF

I like to wear triangular scarves, but I often have too much material at my neck and not enough at the ends. I also like to wear rectangular scarves, but I often have too many wraps around my neck and not the right amount of material in the ends.

So, why not a scarf that combines the best of both ... that offers a triangle with just the right coverage at the neck and with ends just the right size? Well, why not indeed!

This is now my very favorite scarf. I have at least four of them, and I am always knitting one as a gift. They are nifty small projects that you can knit in any yarn, and they can be worn in many ways.

Here's how!

With e-wrap cast-on (page 10), cast on 3 stitches (sts).
If you really hate the e-wrap, then use the knitted cast-on (page 18), but work it very loosely. The long-tail cast-on will not work.
Knit (k) 3 sts.
*Turn. Cast 3 sts onto left-hand needle.
K all sts.
Repeat from* until there are 117 sts on needle.
1 Turn. Cast 49 sts onto left-hand needle.
K 166 sts.
2 Turn. Cast 49 sts onto left-hand needle—215 sts on needle.

EXPERIENCE
• *beginner's first project*
• *minimal shaping*

10cm/4"

12-13
10-13
• *over garter stitches and ridges*
• *after blocking or pressing*

You'll need

1 2 3 4 **5** 6

• *bulky weight*
• *250 yds*
• *novelty yarn, especially ribbon*

I used

• *6mm/US 10, 60cm/24"*

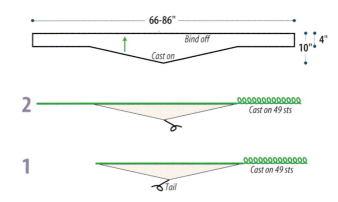

46 ◆ T H E   K N I T T I N G   E X P E R I E N C E ◆

K all sts until straight ends are 4" tall.
Bind off loosely.
Sew in tails (page 39).
Block, or press with steam iron on wool setting.

> *Despite what the labels say, if you are using a ribbon yarn, I recommend that you press heavily and on both sides. This changes the fabric into something quite luscious, and it may be a lumpy and unlovely thing if you don't.*

3 balls TRENDSETTER Dune in color #54

3 balls GREAT ADIRONDACK YARN CO. Caribe Irisee in color Leopard

3 balls NORO Silk Garden in color #47

KNIT-ROUND SCARF

The idea for this piece came while knitting a traditional yoke sweater. (A yoke sweater is one in which the entire upper body of the sweater is knit circularly, as one piece, with decreases for the shoulders and neck.)

I looked at it and wondered, "What if we do just the yoke? Haven't I seen something like that in some glitzy fashion magazine?" This was a piece where I didn't know how it would work … or if it would work … then it was done … and I was thrilled with the result!

And then Rick Mondragon (editor of Knitter's) imagined it modeled as a skirt! Amazing!

There are two pieces shown here, knit in different yarns and different colorways. Even though the same numbers of stitches were used (and I used the same size needles for both pieces), they knit up—and then pressed out—to different circumferences. Hence the two sizes shown. Here is what you can expect:
- *a lighter medium weight yarn will produce a 48" circumference*
- *a heavier medium weight yarn will produce a 51" circumference*

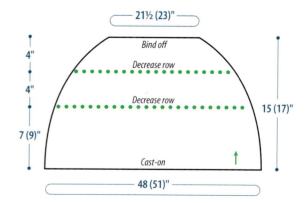

But since you don't yet know how to produce this fabric other than by knitting in rounds, you can't yet knit a small, flat gauge swatch. And you will have done a lot of knitting before you can check your gauge. So here is where I get to say the rarest of things: "Don't worry about a gauge swatch! Just go for it! It'll fit!" The pattern anticipates different circumferences and tells you what to do.

Here's how!

With a 3-yd tail and using long-tail cast-on (page 58), cast on 180 stitches (sts).

Place marker onto right-hand needle.

Form circle with needle, being careful not to twist cast-on (page 61).

Knit (k) sts from left- onto right-hand needle.

Continue to k all sts, in rounds (rnds; pages 58-61), slipping marker from left- to right-hand needle each time (to mark beginnings of rnds).

Don't be alarmed that the piece rolls up as you knit. Most of the roll will be removed at the end.

• If your piece is knitting to the smaller circumference, knit the shorter length. It'll fit your neck and shoulders.

• If your piece is knitting to the larger circumference, knit the longer length. It'll cover your arms to your elbows . . . and if it fits as a skirt . . . congrats to you!

Work in rnds to 7 (9)" from beginning, ending at marker.

1st decrease rnd *K2, knit 2 together (k2tog, page 57), repeat from*, ending at marker—135 sts on needle.

K all sts, in rnds, to 11 (13)" from beginning, ending at marker.

2nd decrease rnd *K1, k2tog, k2tog, repeat from*, ending at marker—81 sts on needle.

K all sts, in rnds, to 15 (17)" from beginning, ending at marker.

If you run out of yarn a little short of this, don't buy more! Just finish as follows.

Bind off loosely *(very loosely for skirt).*

Sew in tails (page 39).

To flatten and achieve final measurements, wash, then pin flat to dry.

Knit-round worn as a skirt: 5 balls NATURALLY Café in color #715

EXPERIENCE
• *beginner's first project*
• *minimal shaping*

10cm/4"

14-15
• *over stockinette stitch*
• *knit in rounds*

You'll need
1 2 3 **4** 5 6

• *medium weight*
• *330 (400) yds*
• *anything*

I used

• *5mm/US 8,
40–60cm/16–24"*

LEGWARMERS:
MAXIMUM & MINIMUM

EXPERIENCE

Minimum legwarmers
- **beginner's first project**
- **minimal shaping**

EXPERIENCE

Maximum legwarmers
- **very easy**
- **minimal shaping through color changes**

10cm/4"

22•24
14•16

- **over stockinette stitch**
- **knit in rounds**
- **14 sts for Maximum**
- **16 sts for Minimum**

You'll need

1 2 3 **4** 5 6

- **medium weight**
- **220 (400) yds**
- **soft wool or wool blend**

I used

- **5 (5.5)mm/US 8 (9), 35-40cm/14-16"**

The terms 'maximum' and 'minimum' refer to both impact and size. The larger Maximum legwarmers are the most can't-miss-'em piece in this book: the smaller Minimum legwarmers are something even the most sedate of us can carry off. Having said that, there's no reason the larger pair can't be knit in one color or the smaller in many colors. The pattern is written so you have choices.

All instructions are for both styles: Minimum first, then Maximum. Different needle sizes and different yarns produce the different circumferences.
Measure your first leg warmer after a few inches.
- If it matches the Maximum circumference, follow directions for that size.
- If it matches the Minimum circumference, follow directions for that size.

Maximum legwarmers: 4 balls NORO Kureyon, 2 in color #75 and 2 in color #57 (Each ball is already a blend of many colors.)

(stretches to 12)"

10"

Bind off

Decreases

14"

Minimum

Cast on

12"
(stretches to 16)"

(stretches to 13)"

11"

Bind off

Decreases

24"

Maximum

Cast on

14"
(stretches to 18)"

Here's how!

UPPER LEG

With 36" tail, and using long-tail cast-on (page 58), cast on 50 stitches (sts).

These can be knit on a set of five double-pointed needles (page 60)—if the right size circular is not available, or if you find it uncomfortable, or if the knitting becomes too stretched. Cast all 50 stitches onto one needle, then distribute onto four needles: 12 stitches on 1st and 3rd needles, 13 stitches on 2nd and 4th needles.

Place marker onto right-hand needle.

Form circle with needle, being careful not to twist cast-on (page 61). Knit (k) sts from left-hand needle onto right-hand needle, slipping marker each time to designate beginning of rounds (rnds; pages 58-61).

For single-color legwarmers: K in rnds to 10 (14)" from cast-on.

For multicolor legwarmers: K in rnds to 1" from cast-on. Do not cut 1st color; leave hanging on bumpy/wrong side (WS) of legwarmers.

At marker, begin 2nd color, leaving 4" tail hanging to WS. K with 2nd color for 2 to 7 rnds. Do not cut 2nd color. *At marker, change back to previous color, bringing yarn up WS, without pulling so tight as to pucker or so loosely as to leave holes. K with this color for 2 to 7 rnds.

Try to balance your use of the two colors so you don't run out of either.

Repeat from* to 10 (14)" from beginning, ending at marker.

CALF SHAPING

Begin shaping immediately after marker. (For multicolor legwarmers, continue color changes through shaping.)

1st decrease rnd K10, knit 2 together (k2tog, page 57), k11, k2tog, k10, k2tog, k11, k2tog. (You should now be at marker—46 sts on needle.)

Work 2" without decreasing, ending at marker.

2nd decrease rnd K9, k2tog, k10, k2tog, k9, k2tog, k10, k2tog. (You should now be at marker—42 sts on needle.)

Work 2" without decreasing, ending at marker.

For Minimum legwarmers only: Bind off loosely.

For Maximum legwarmers only: ***3rd decrease rnd*** K8, k2tog, k9, k2tog, k8, k2tog, k9, k2tog. (You should now be at marker—38 sts on needle.)

Without further decreasing, work to 24" from beginning. Bind off loosely.

For both: Sew in tails (page 39) to bumpy side.

Now make a second legwarmer, exactly as the first.

For multicolor legwarmers: You may begin the 2nd legwarmer with the same color as the first: you may try to match the stripes . . . or not! The two pieces will go together, however you work them. For Maximum legwarmers: If loose on leg, wear with elastic under the top edge.

Minimum legwarmers: 1 skein CASCADE 220 in color #9412

Medium: 1 skein CASCADE 220 in color #9412

MOSTLY KNIT-ROUND HAT

I had tried to teach my daughter, Caddy, to knit for many years. Somehow, it just didn't stick. But then, one night in her 24th year, something happened!

We—her boyfriend, Andy, my husband, Chris, and Chris's daughter, Sarah—were sitting around, waiting for Caddy to get home from work. I asked one and all, "What shall we do?" Chris said, "It's time for the guys to learn to knit!" So, I taught Andy and Chris while Sarah worked on her poncho.

Caddy came home, saw the spectacle of everyone knitting, sat beside Andy, and said, "I can do that! Let me do some!" And she did!

Then, the first thing she wanted to knit on her own was a hat …and here's the pattern I developed especially for her.

This hat is mostly knit round 'cause it has a garter stitch edging. The reason for this is so you can knit a flat gauge swatch in garter stitch and know the hat will fit.

Here's how!

EDGING

1 With circular needle and your preferred cast-on (I used the e-wrap, page 10), cast on 70 (80, 90) stitches (sts).
Working back and forth, knit (k) all sts for 1".
Next (increase) rnd: *K19, knit in front and back of next stitch (kf&b, page 56), repeat from* 2 (3, 3) times more, k10 (0, 10)—73 (84, 94) sts on needle. Do not turn work at end of row.

BODY

Form a circle with the needle, being careful not to twist knitting.
Place marker onto right-hand needle.
K all sts from left- onto right-hand needle. At the marker, you have knit one round (rnd).
Continue to k all sts, in rnds (pages 58-61), slipping marker from left- to right-hand needle each time (to mark beginning of rnds) to 5 (6, 7)" from beginning (with edging not flipped up), ending at marker.

CROWN

Begin to work onto double-pointed needles (page 60) as follows:

1st (decrease) rnd

All sizes: Onto Needle 1, *k10, place marker, k9, knit two together (k2tog, page 57).*
Onto Needle 2, work *to*.
Onto Needle 3, work *to*.
Small size only: Onto Needle 4, k10.
Medium size only: Onto Needle 4, work *to*.
Large size only: Onto Needle 4, work *to*, place marker, k10.

All sizes: Replace beginning-of-rnd marker with a safety pin in the knitting, and work as follows.
2nd (decrease) rnd On all needles, k to 2 sts before markers, k2tog, k to 2 sts from end of needle, k2tog.
3rd rnd K all sts.
Repeat 2nd and 3rd rnds until 14 (16, 18) sts remain.
Final rnd K2tog for entire rnd, removing markers and working sts from 1st and 2nd needle onto 1st needle and sts from 3rd and 4th needles onto 3rd needle.
Cut tail to 5". Thread onto tapestry needle, and draw through all sts. Pull tight to close.
Use cast-on tail to sew small seam along garter st edging (ridges to ridges, page 42).
Sew in tails (page 39).

The edging on this hat will naturally fold up. This gives you two choices for wearing. With the edging flipped up, it is shorter; with the edging flipped down, it will cover more of the ears.
If you want the edging to not flip, wet the edging (by spraying with water), then pin the edging down and to itself (front to back) around the hat. Let dry.

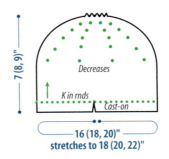

7 (8, 9)"

Decreases

K in rnds

Cast-on

16 (18, 20)"
stretches to 18 (20, 22)"

1 Increase row
K flat (garter stitch)

EXPERIENCE

- *beginner's first project*
  - *minimal shaping*
  - *minimal finishing*

It'll fit

S (M, L)

10cm/4"

 GET CLOSE

17-18

- *over garter stitches*

You'll need

1 2 3 **4** 5 6

- *medium weight*
- *100 (110, 130) yds*
  - *soft wool or wool blend*

I used

- *4.5mm/US 7 40cm/16"*

- *4.5mm/US 7*

1 skein MOUNTAIN COLORS 4/8's Wool in color Mountain Twilight

MOUNTAIN COLORS 4/8's Wool in color Bitterroot Rainbow

KNIT-FLAT HAT AND MITTS

Hats are easy enough to knit, either on circulars or on double-pointed needles, because the circumferences are fairly large. But once we work on mitts, their smaller circumference—especially for the thumb—makes the piece a whole lot more difficult.

What to do for a beginner who wants matching hat and mitts? My solution is to knit them both flat and suggest you knit the hat first. Even so, the mitts are still much more challenging than the hat.

Here's how!

HAT

With your preferred cast-on (I used the e-wrap, page 10), cast on 110 stitches (sts). Knit (k) all sts, all rows, to 5" from beginning (or to desired height).

> *The hat shown is knit to a height of 5". It covers an adult head—forehead and ears. You could knit to a height of 4", covering the forehead but not much of the ears. Or you could knit to a height of 3", for one of those cute little flat-tops, covering only a little forehead and none of the ears. You'll use much less yarn for the latter!*

Determine right side (RS) of cast-on, then end with next wrong-side (WS) row.

CROWN

1st decrease row (RS) K1, *k10, knit two together (k2tog, page 57), place marker; repeat from* 8 times more and to 1 st remaining, k1— 101 sts on needle.

Next 3 rows K all sts.

2nd decrease row (RS) K1, *k to 2 sts before marker, k2tog, repeat from* 8 times more and to 1 st remaining, k1.

Next 3 rows K all sts.

Repeat last 4 rows until 20 sts remain.

Last decrease row K1, *k2tog, repeat from* 8 times more and to 1 st remaining, k 1—11 sts on needle. Cut tail to 10". Thread onto tapestry needle and draw through remaining 11 sts. Pull tight to close. Sew center back seam (ridges to ridges, page 42). Sew in tails (page 39).

EXPERIENCE
Hat

- **beginner's first project**
  - **minimal shaping**
  - **minimal finishing**

EXPERIENCE
Mitts

- **easy intermediate**
- **mid-level shaping**
- **mid-level finishing**

It'll fit
most adults

10cm/4"

20 GET CLOSE

20

- **over garter stitches and ridges**

You'll need

1 2 3 **4** 5 6

- **medium weight**
- **150 yds for hat**
- **200 yds for mitts**
  - **soft wool or wool blend**

I used

- **4mm/US 6**

MITTS

1 CUFF

With your preferred cast-on (I used the e-wrap, page 10), cast on 32 stitches (sts).
Knit (k) all sts, all rows, to approximately 2".
Determine right side (RS) of cast-on, then end with next wrong-side (WS) row.

2 PALM

1st increase row (RS) K1, knit in front and back of next stitch (kf&b, page 57), k12, kf&b, k2, kf&b, k12, kf&b, k1—36 sts on needle.
Next 3 rows K all sts.
2nd increase row (RS) K1, kf&b, k14, kf&b, k2, kf&b, k14, kf&b, k1—40 sts on needle
Next 3 rows K all sts.

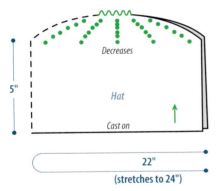

Decreases

Hat

Cast on

5"

22"
(stretches to 24")

3rd increase row (RS) K1, kf&b, k to 2 sts remaining, kf&b, k1—42 sts on needle.
Next 3 rows K all sts.
Repeat last 4 rows 6 times more—54 sts on needle. At beginning of next RS row, break yarn, leaving 4-yd tail for thumb.

3 FINGERS AREA

With RS facing, put first 7 sts onto holder for thumb, re-attach yarn and k40, put remaining 7 sts onto second holder for thumb.
K40 sts to 4" past sts left for thumb.

4 *1st decrease row (RS)* *K3, knit two together (k2tog, page 57), repeat from* 7 times more—32 sts on needle.
All following WS rows K all sts.
2nd decrease row (RS) *K2, k2tog, repeat from* 7 times more—24 sts on needle.
3rd decrease row (RS) *K1, k2tog, repeat from* 7 times more—16 sts on needle.
4th decrease row (RS) K2tog across row—8 sts on needle. K1 WS row.

5 Cut yarn, leaving 12" tail (long enough to seam down fingers-area opening). Thread onto tapestry needle, and draw through all sts. Pull tight to close. Sew fingers-area seam (stitches to ridges, page 42).

6 THUMB

With RS facing, put all 14 sts for thumb onto one needle, ready to work RS row beginning at open edge. K all sts for 2 rows (paying attention to their orientation, page 146, on first row).
1st (increase) row (RS) K1, kf&b, k to 2 sts remaining, kf&b, k1—16 sts on needle.
K all sts to desired height for thumb (1½–1¾").
Final row (RS) K2tog across row—8 sts on needle.
Thread remaining yarn onto tapestry needle, and draw through all sts. Pull tight to close.
Sew down open edge of thumb, palm, and cuff.
Sew in tails (page 39).
Make a second mitt, exactly as the first.

To designate right and left mitts, put one mitt on right hand, then take it off carefully so you maintain the shape it takes. Press it lightly with a steam iron.
Do the same with the left.

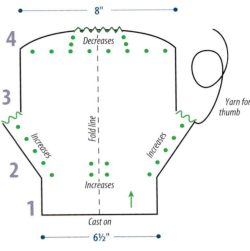

8"

Decreases

Fold line

Increases

Increases

Increases

Yarn for thumb

Cast on

6½"

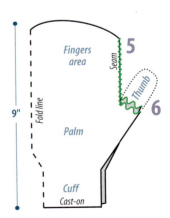

Fingers area

Seam

Thumb

Fold line

9"

Palm

Cuff
Cast-on

Front and back *F B*

In garments, and on the body, there is a *front* and a *back*. In a row of knitting, and in the stitches themselves, there is also a front and a back.

When clearly not speaking about garment (body) pieces, the terms front and back mean the following.
- The *front* of your knitting is the side of the knitting that is facing you, as you are working, even if you are on a wrong-side row.
- The *back* of your knitting is the side of the knitting that is away from you, as you are working, whether you are on a right- or a wrong-side row.

As you knit, note that when you are working a knit stitch, your yarn is to the back.

Knitting into the front or back of a stitch *kf kb*

In the Oops! chapter, one of the first things you are told is that you can knit into the back of a stitch to untwist one that is backwards. See page 146.

When you work a knit stitch, you put your right-hand needle into the side of the stitch closest to you—the front of the stitch.

If you were to put your right-hand needle into the side of the stitch away from you, you would be knitting into the back of the stitch.

Working straight

Sometimes patterns tell you to *work straight* for a particular distance or to a particular length. This just means to work without increases or decreases or shaping of any kind. (This is also referred to as *working even.)*

Working a decrease *dec*

When you make one stitch from two, you are *decreasing*. There are many ways to do this: one is presented here, another will be explored in a subsequent chapter.

KNITTING TWO STITCHES TOGETHER *k2tog*
Knitting two stitches together is the easiest of decreases. It produces a decrease that slants to the right.

Oops! I forgot to work a decrease! What do I do now? See page 150.

Oops! I misplaced my decrease! What do I do now? See page 150.

1 Put right-hand needle into first two stitches on left-hand needle, beginning with the second stitch from the end of the left-hand needle.

2 Knit both stitches together, as if they were one stitch, and you've made a decrease!

Working an increase *inc*

When you make two stitches from one, you are *increasing*. There are many ways to do this: one is presented here, another will be explored in a subsequent chapter.

KNITTING INTO THE FRONT AND BACK OF A STITCH *kf&b*
When directions tell you to *knit into the front and back,* they mean for you to do both in the same stitch. This increase works very well in garter stitch.

Oops! I forgot to work an increase! What do I do now? See page 150.

1 Knit into the front of the stitch, as usual, but do not pull the stitch off the left-hand needle.

2 Take right-hand needle to back, and put it through the back of the same stitch.

3 Knit as usual…

4 …and you've made an increase!

The long-tail cast-on

Here's a flexible cast-on that is a good choice when working circularly (although it can be used for flat knitting also). It's really just the e-wrap with a row of knitting attached, but it's easier to manage than the e-wrap, since the stitches don't fall off the needle as readily.

1 Leave a tail 2.5 times the width of the piece for which you are casting on. Put right-hand needle under yarn at this point. Tail is to front, yarn is to back, and right index finger is holding yarn against right-hand needle.

2 Put left thumb under tail.

3 Put left index finger under yarn.

4 Hold both tail and yarn in left palm.

Knitting in rounds

KNITTING IN ROUNDS: THE THEORETICAL STUFF

Here's some basic information that will help you understand what follows.

- When you knit a stitch, you pull the new stitch through the old, pushing the loop of the old stitch to the back of the work. This produces a *bump* that sits on the back.

Garter stitch is what you've learned so far, and here is what it's about.

- In garter stitch, you knit one row (pushing the bumps to the 'wrong side'), then turn and knit another row (pushing the bumps to the 'right side').
- Turning at the end of every row, and pushing the bumps to alternate sides, produces the evenly textured, ridged fabric of garter stitch and a flat piece of knitting.

But you can also *knit in rounds,* and here's what this is about.

- Knitting in rounds, and always pushing the bumps to the same side, produces a fabric with an all-smooth side and an all-bumpy side and a tubular piece of knitting.

The result of knitting back and forth is a flat piece of knitting and the textured fabric of garter stitch.

A fabric with a smooth side and a bumpy side can also be produced by knitting flat—back and forth, turning the work at the ends of rows. But the wrong-side rows would not be knit, they would be purled (something you will learn in Book 2 of *The Knitting Experience.*)

The result of knitting in-the-round is a tubular piece of knitting, with a smooth side and a bumpy side.

5 Insert tip of right-hand needle into front of tail (on thumb).

6 Take needle over top of yarn (on index finger), then around the back and under.

7 Draw yarn through the loop on the thumb.

8 Pull both tail and yarn to tighten cast-on stitch. (There are now two stitches on right-hand needle.)

Repeat Steps 5–8 until required number of stitches is on right-hand needle. Try to maintain uniform spacing between cast-on stitches.

For some patterns, it will be important to recognize that with long-tail cast-on you have already worked Row 1.

Here is a photo showing how to recognize stitches and rows in stockinette stitch. (The horizontal is a row shown over 9 stitches; the vertical is a stitch shown over 8 rows.)

Stockinette and *St st*
reverse stockinette *rev St st*

The name of the smooth side of the fabric, produced by knitting in rounds, is stockinette stitch; the name of the bumpy side is reverse stockinette stitch. The smooth side is usually the right side, but there are garments for which the bumpy side is chosen as the right side (and there are some in this chapter).

Circular needles come in a range of lengths—from 12" to 36" and beyond. There is not much demand for the larger sizes, and I find the 12" length cramp-inducing. Most of the work you do on circulars can be adequately managed on 16–24" lengths. And remember that you can work flat, turning at the end of each row, on a circular needle of any length.

Working with double-pointed needles is the knitting where you look like you really know what you're doing, 'cause you work with a lap full of needles! (You still only knit with two needles at a time, but don't tell anyone.)

Double-pointed needles can also come in many lengths—from 4½" to 12". Most of the work you do on double-pointed needles can be adequately managed on the 6–7" length. But do use the least slippery ones you can so they don't fall out of your knitting too easily.

When using double-pointed needles, I prefer to use sets of five rather than sets of four. Why? Because a circle formed by four needles is easier to manage than a circle formed by three. And it is often the case that our patterns are more easily divided into four segments than into three. If you only have a set of four, just combine the stitches of the third and fourth needles onto one needle: this becomes your third needle. Our fifth needle becomes your fourth.

KNITTING IN ROUNDS: THE PRACTICAL STUFF

Knitting in rounds is easy! No seams, just round and round. What could go wrong? Well, you'll get into a muddle if you don't pay attention to
  • choosing the right needles,
  • not knitting over a twisted cast-on,
  • marking where the beginning of a round is.
All of these issues are addressed in what follows.

KNITTING IN ROUNDS ON CIRCULAR NEEDLES

To knit in rounds, you may use a circular needle. The circumference of the piece you are knitting (given in the pattern) should be close to the length of the circular needle you use (measured from tip to tip).

But what happens when the circumference of the piece is too small for a circular? You need to use something else, and the choice I prefer is switching to double-pointed needles.

KNITTING IN ROUNDS ON DOUBLE-POINTED NEEDLES *dpns*

Here's how to work in-the-round with five double-pointed needles.

1 Find the beginning of the round. It is designated in this series of photos by a red marker. Yours might be identifiable by the tail of the cast-on. The needles are always numbered by their position relative to the beginning of the round.

Looking clockwise, the first needle to the left of the marker is Needle 1 (shown here in the left hand), the next needle (at the upper left of the circle) is Needle 2. The next needle (at the upper right of the circle and shown here in the right hand) is Needle 3, and the last needle (to the right of the marker) is Needle 4. The fifth needle is the remaining needle, free of stitches. It becomes your 'right-hand needle.'

USING STITCH MARKERS

Stitch markers help you keep track of where you are in your knitting and can save you from repeated counting.

A marker sits on your needle between two stitches and stays in that same place in your knitting for a number of rows. When you come to a marker, just slip it from the left- to the right-hand needle.

CAST-ON FOR KNITTING IN ROUNDS

Here's how to be sure you do not begin knitting in rounds with a twisted cast-on.
- Cast on all stitches.
- Look at the cast-on and make sure all stitches sit on top of the needle, the cast-on edge is at the bottom, and the cast-on doesn't spiral around the needle.
- Put right-hand needle into first stitch on left-hand needle.
- Before knitting, check again to make sure the cast-on is not twisted.

In the Knit-Flat Hat pattern in this chapter, you need to decrease at the same place every time, nine times in every other row. By placing markers that divide the work into nine segments, you only have to work to the marker, and then you'll be told how to work your decrease.

Patterns for which markers are helpful usually tell you where and when to place them.

If you knit over a twisted cast-on, you'll produce a twisted piece of fabric that cannot be untwisted.

2 As you begin the round, Needle 1 becomes your 'left-hand needle.' You will knit stitches from Needle 1 onto the free needle.

3 As stitches are knit onto the free needle, it becomes Needle 1 (because it is the first needle to the left of the marker that designates the beginning of the round).

Soon you will have a new free needle. It becomes your 'right-hand needle,' and Needle 2 becomes your 'left-hand needle'.

And that's all there is to it. You continue clockwise, knitting the old stitches onto a free needle, until you have a new free needle. But do remember when working a pattern that needles are always numbered by their position relative to the beginning of the round.

ATTENTION TO DETAIL

Throughout this series, special attention is paid to the details that will make your work look well-executed. Just because the piece is easy to knit doesn't mean it has to look like it was done by a novice. "God is in the details" has been a guiding principle.

Sometimes the detail comes at the beginning of your project. In Chapter 3, you are taught the crochet cast-on. If you use it, all your edges will match.

The crochet cast-on is not an easy thing to master. I have heard advanced knitters say, "You can't teach that to a beginner! It's too difficult!" Well, it's not difficult if you don't have much to compare it with. Besides, there's lots about knitting that's difficult. But it's often these taxing little touches that make the work look perfectly executed—like using a method for casting on that matches the bind-off.

Sometimes attention to detail is needed throughout the project. In Chapter 4, you maintain a slip stitch at the edges of all pieces.

I remember reading a book about Buddhists (but that's all the reference I can offer), in which there was a young man who kept pestering the elder, "Tell me the secret to life." The elder refused, for some time, before finally answering, "Pay attention."

There are notes in the patterns of Chapter 4, telling you how important it is to pay attention to your slip-stitch edge. There will be other directives in other knitting patterns . . . as there will be moments in life . . . when paying attention is essential. Wouldn't it be wonderful if we always had notes to point them out!

And sometimes the attention to detail comes at the end of the piece. Throughout this book, you are taught what is required to assemble your garments well.

There are many knitters who love the knitting but hate the seaming. They get to the finishing directions and retreat. I think it's because 'we don't love what we don't understand.' We learn one method of seaming and don't realize that it doesn't apply to all situations. Most patterns do not offer detailed seaming instruction. So if the only method we know is inappropriate, the result is sloppy. What's to love about this?!

A student of mine once said, "No matter how much money you've spent on the yarn or how much time you've spent knitting, it's what you do in the last two hours that makes all the difference!" She was right: perfectly wonderful knitting has been ruined by awkward finishing.

"God is in the details." One of the central tenets of this book is to help you attend to the details.

When I initially made the Best-friend Jacket, I knew I was doing the first piece of knitting for this book, but I didn't know where the idea of the asymmetry came from, and I didn't know if it would work. The results were astounding.

What happened the first time I wore it was that everyone commented on it . . . and most everyone wanted one. Why? Sure, the simple shape is appealing, the yarn is gorgeous, and since nothing is the same length it's difficult to make a mistake! But there was something else going on. What was it?

Here's what I think . . . and what I learned when I taught my creativity class with this jacket as a demonstration piece.

To 10% of the world, the asymmetry of this garment is like fingernails on a chalk-board. To the other 90%, the asymmetry of this garment is exciting. Why? I often joke, "If it's asymmetrical, it's art!" But I think there's more going on than this.

I think it speaks to our brain hemispheres. The left (and usually dominant) likes order and symmetry; the right is enthused by the off-beat. Those who are entrenched in the left brain can't tolerate asymmetry: these are the 10% who look at this garment and say, "Whaaat, you didn't have enough yarn?" But most of us, even though left-brain dominant, welcome the opportunity to get into the right; these are the 90% who look at this garment and say, "I want one!"

The Asymmetrical Vest came later. I designed it for those who 'want one' but without the commitment of time and money that the jacket demands. But while the vest takes less time and less yarn, it is actually a more difficult project than the jacket because it has more shaping. (As you continue on your knitting journey, you'll find lots of factors to complicate your knitting . . . and shaping is one of them.)

Chapter Three

The Patterns

Additional Skills

EXPERIENCE
- *very easy*
- *minimal shaping*
- *minimal finishing*
- *lots of knitting*

OVERSIZED FIT

S (M, L, XL, XXL)

A 44 (48, 52, 56, 60)"
B **Back length:** knit to 25 (25½, 26, 26½, 27)", stretches to 27–29"
C knit to 28", stretches to 29"

10cm/4"

13 **GET GAUGE!**
13

- *over garter stitches and ridges*

You'll need

1 2 3 4 **5** 6

- *bulky weight*
- *1100 (1150, 1300, 1425, 1550) yds*
- *something interesting, with a little weight*

- *3 or 4 large buttons or toggles*

I used

- *6.5mm/US 10½, 60cm/24"*

- *5.5/US 9*

- *6.5mm/US K*

Medium: 22 skeins CLASSIC ELITE Zoom in color #1058

BEST-FRIEND JACKET

I named this the Best-friend Jacket because it always makes you feel good, always makes you look good, always comes through for you when you don't know what to wear. In addition, most of my best friends have chosen to make one!

This piece is knit side to side, and sometimes it's tough to understand what you're doing. Check out the accompanying drawings, to help you get your bearings. But you'll also see both fronts and the back are different lengths, so … if you get something wrong … who's to know?!

Speaking of length, if you prefer a shorter style don't hesitate to make this garment shorter; it'll still look wonderful. (The blue version, page 68, is an inch and a half shorter than the rust; you'll see how to do this in the pattern.)

The rust version is made in an alpaca blend. Alpaca is a wonderful fiber, but the knitted fabric is heavy. In a side-to-side garment, this will most affect sleeve length. (See Measuring length, page 79, to be sure your sleeves won't be too long.)

Here's how!

1 LEFT CUFF

With crochet cast-on (page 74), cast on 28 (28, 34, 34, 34) sts onto smaller needle.
Knit (k) 1 right-side (RS) row. Turn work. Hang marker on side of knitting facing you: this designates wrong side (WS) of fabric. Continue to move marker up knitting, as needed.
K all stitches (sts), all rows, to 6 ridges (ending with WS row).

2 LEFT SLEEVE

Next row (RS) K4, *make 1 (M1, page 79), k3, repeat from* 6 (6, 8, 8, 8) times more, M1, k3—36 (36, 44, 44, 44) sts on needle.
Change to larger needle(s).
K 3 rows.
Next (increase) row (RS) K1, M1, k to 1 st remaining, M1, k1.
Repeat last 4 rows (increasing at each end every 4th row) to 72 (72, 78, 78, 78) sts. At final increase, hang marker on edge of piece.

> *You'll need to know where this place is when you knit the right sleeve to match.*

Continue to k all sts, all rows, without increases, to 17 (16, 15, 14, 13)" from beginning of sleeve or to desired sleeve length, ending with WS row. SHORTEN OR LENGTHEN Sleeve here.

3 LEFT BACK AND FRONT

> *If you wish to SHORTEN OR LENGTHEN Back and Front here, make a photocopy of the accompanying drawings; you will record numbers on them.*

With RS facing and with crochet hook, draw yarn through first st on left-hand needle. Work crochet cast-on to 45 (47, 45, 47, 49) sts cast-on—117 (119, 123, 125, 127) sts on needle. SHORTEN OR LENGTHEN Left Back here.

> *To shorten by 1", cast on 3 fewer sts. To lengthen by 1", cast on 3 more sts. Where you see A___ on your photocopy, record the number of sts more (+3?) or less (-3?) that you cast on for the Left Back. For the blue version, A=-4.*

K 1 (RS) row. Turn work.

With WS facing and with crochet hook, draw yarn through first st on left-hand needle. Work crochet cast-on to 32 (34, 32, 34, 36) sts cast-on—149 (153, 155, 159, 163) sts on needle. SHORTEN OR LENGTHEN Left Front here.

> *To shorten by 1", cast on 3 fewer sts. To lengthen by 1", cast on 3 more sts. Where you see B___ on your photocopy, record the number of sts more (+3?) or less (-3?) that you cast on for the Left Front. For the blue version, B=-4.*

For the body of the garment, I suggest working all rows as follows: with yarn in front (yf, page 76), slip first st purl-wise (sl 1 p-wise, page 78), take yarn to back (yb), k to end of row. (This slip-st edge will make your edges neater and make the garment hang nicely.) Work to 7½ (8½, 9½, 10½, 11½)" from Left Back and Front cast-on edge, ending with WS row.

> *Don't forget to keep moving your marker (designating the WS) up your work, as needed.*

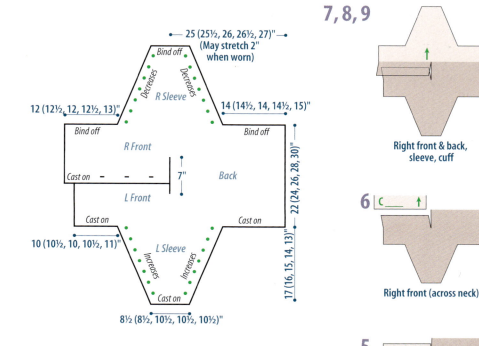

— 25 (25½, 26, 26½, 27)"→
(May stretch 2" when worn)

Bind off

Decreases *Decreases*

R Sleeve

12 (12½, 12, 12½, 13)"   14 (14½, 14, 14½, 15)"

Bind off   *Bind off*

R Front

Cast on - - -   7"   *Back*

L Front

Cast on   *Cast on*

22 (24, 26, 28, 30)"

10 (10½, 10, 10½, 11)"

L Sleeve

Increases *Increases*

17 (16, 15, 14, 13)"

Cast on

8½ (8½, 10½, 10½, 10½)"

4 CENTER BACK (ACROSS NECK)

K 81 (83, 84, 86, 88) sts. Slip remaining 68 (70, 71, 73, 75) sts onto a holder.

> *Both these stitch counts will be different if you altered lengths of Left Back and Front. See A___ and B___ on your photocopy, to see what your numbers should be.*

Turn work. Continue over Back sts only to 7" from beginning of Center Back section, ending with WS row. Break yarn.

Put these sts on a holder.

5 LEFT FRONT (ACROSS NECK)

Return to sts on needle or holder, ready to work RS row. Work to 5" from beginning of Left Front section, ending with WS row.

Bind off.

7, 8, 9

Right front & back, sleeve, cuff

6 C___ ↑

Right front (across neck)

5 ↑

Left front (across neck)

4 ↑

Center back (across neck)

1, 2, 3 B___   A___ ↑

Left cuff, sleeve, back & front

Medium: 4 skeins SCHAEFER YARNS Elaine in color Eleanor Roosevelt

6 RIGHT FRONT (ACROSS NECK)

With crochet cast-on, cast on 74 (76, 78, 80, 82) sts onto larger needle. SHORTEN OR LENGTHEN Right Front here.

To shorten by 1", cast on 3 fewer sts. To lengthen by 1", cast on 3 more sts. Where you see C___ on your photocopy, record the number of sts more (+3?) or less (-3?) that you cast on for Right Front. For the blue version, C=-4.

Work 1 (RS) row.

Turn work. Hang marker on side of knitting facing you: this designates WS of fabric. Continue to move marker up knitting, as needed.

Work this piece also with a sl st at the beginning of all rows.

Work to 3 ridges, ending with WS row.

Next row (begin buttonholes, RS) Yf, sl 1 p-wise, yb, k5, *yarn over (yo, page 77), knit two together (k2tog, page 57), k14, repeat from* twice more, yo, k2tog, k to end. Four buttonholes made.

Next row (end buttonholes) Yf, sl 1 p-wise, yb, k to end, knitting through back of yo's (to tighten them, page 77).

Continue to 5" from beginning of Right Front section, ending with WS row.

Break yarn.

7 RIGHT FRONT AND BACK

Slip sts from Center Back holder onto left-hand needle, continuous with sts of Right Front, ready to work RS row—155 (159, 162, 166, 170) sts on needle.

This stitch count will be different if you altered lengths of Left Back and Right Front. See A___ and C___ on your photocopy, to see what your number should be.

Join yarn and work to 7½ (8½, 9½, 10½, 11½)" from beginning of Right Front and Back, ending with WS row.

Next row (RS) Bind off 45 (47, 45, 47, 49) sts at beginning of row.

Bind off more or less, if you altered length: see A___.

Next row (WS) Bind off 38 (40, 39, 41, 43) sts at beginning of row—72 (72, 78, 78, 78) sts on needle.

Bind off more or less, if you altered length: see C___.

8 RIGHT SLEEVE

Do not work sl sts at edges beyond this point.
K all sts to same number of garter ridges that you worked beyond last increase on Left Sleeve, ending with WS row.

This is the number of ridges between marker and armhole on Left Sleeve.

Next decrease row (RS) K1, sl1, k1, pass slip st over (SKP, page 79), k to 3 sts remaining, k2tog.
K 3 rows.

Repeat last 4 rows (decreasing at each end every 4th row) to 36 (36, 44, 44, 44) sts.

Next row (RS) K3, *k2tog, k2, repeat from* 6 (6, 8, 8, 8) times more, k2tog, k3—28 (28, 34, 34, 34) sts on needle.

9 RIGHT CUFF

Change back to smaller needle(s), k 6 ridges.
Bind off.

FINISHING

Remove marker.

Beginning at left cuff, sew left underarm (ridges to ridges, page 42) and side seam (stitches to stitches, page 74) to within 6½" of lower back edge and to within 2½" of lower left front edge.

Beginning at right cuff, sew right underarm and side seam to within 6½" of lower back edge and to within 4½" of lower right front edge.

Sew buttons to Left Front to correspond to buttonholes, placing them 1¼" from bound-off edge. Or, if you prefer to give garment slight A-line shape and for more overlap at neck, sew top button 2½" from edge, second button 2" from edge, third button 1½" from edge, and last button 1" from edge.

I am ambivalent about the fourth buttonhole. The garment might be less structured and more playful without it (see front cover). To remove it may require closing the hole, with some yarn of the garment and on the WS.

EXPERIENCE

- *easy intermediate*
- *mid-level shaping*
- *minimal finishing*

OVERSIZED FIT

S (M, L, XL, XXL)

A 40 (44, 48, 52, 56)"
B Back length: 24"

10cm/4"

9 GET GAUGE!

9

- *over garter stitches and ridges*

You'll need

1 2 3 4 5 **6**

- super bulky weight
- 350 (400, 450, 500, 550) yds
- something soft

- Three 1" buttons

I used

- 8mm/US 11

- 6–7mm/US J–K

Medium: 5 balls STYLECRAFT Fleece in color #3444
Shape it! scarf: 3 skeins GREAT ADIRONDACK YARN CO.
Opera in color Starburst

ASYMMETRICAL VEST

I love vests! There are lots of places you can wear them where you can't wear jackets, plus you have more opportunity to build an outfit 'cause the sleeves of whatever you're wearing underneath contribute.

Here's how!

Before you start, make a photocopy of the accompanying drawings to record numbers on them.
It seems that this garment should not be very challenging: there isn't much to it, the yarn is thick, and none of the edges are supposed to match. (If you cast on or bind off the wrong number of stitches, who's to know!) However, because the yarn is thick, there aren't many stitches or ridges, so you are always doing something in order to accomplish the shaping. Hence the challenge. If you make notes on your photocopy, you'll have an easier time sorting out where you are as you knit.

1 RIGHT FRONT

With crochet cast-on (page 74), cast on 48 stitches (sts). SHORTEN OR LENGTHEN HERE

To shorten by 1", cast on 2–3 fewer sts.
To lengthen by 1", cast on 2–3 more sts.
Where you see A____ on your photocopy, record the number of sts more (+3?) or less (-3?) that you cast on for the Right Front. You will refer to it every time the pattern says, "This number will be different if you altered length."

All following rows (unless otherwise directed) With yarn in front (yf, page 76), slip first st purl-wise (sl 1 p-wise, page 78), take yarn to back (yb), knit (k) to end of row.
The slip-stitch (sl-st) edge will make your edges neater and make the garment hang nicely.
Work 3 more rows, ending with wrong side (WS) row.
Next right side (RS) row (begin buttonholes) Yf, sl 1 p-wise, yb, k11, *yarn over (yo, page 77), knit two together (k2tog, page 57), k6, repeat from* once more, yo, k2tog, k to end. Three buttonholes made.
Next row (end buttonholes) Yf, sl 1 p-wise, yb, k to end, knitting through back of buttonhole yo's (to tighten them, page 77).
Continue to 5½" from beginning, ending with WS row.

2 RIGHT FRONT SHOULDER

The sl-st edge will not be worked at the beginning of some RS rows through the following shoulder and armhole shaping.

Next row (RS) K to end.

Next row (WS) Yf, sl 1 p-wise, yb, k to end.

Repeat these last 2 rows 0 (1, 2, 3, 3) times more.

Row 1 (decrease row, RS) K1, slip 1, knit 1, pass slip stitch over (SKP, page 79), k to end.

Rows 2 & 4 (WS) Yf, sl 1 p-wise, yb, k to end.

Row 3 (RS) K.

Repeat these last 4 rows, ending with row 2, until you have decreased 4 sts at the shoulder and 44 sts remain. (This number will be different if you altered length.)

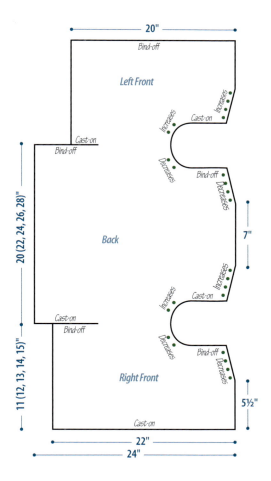

20"
Bind-off
Left Front
Cast-on
Bind-off
Cast-on
Increases
Increases
Cast-on
Decreases
Bind-off
Decreases
Back
7"
20 (22, 24, 26, 28)"
Increases
Cast-on
Increases
Cast-on
Bind-off
Decreases
Bind-off
Decreases
Right Front
11 (12, 13, 14, 15)"
5½"
Cast-on
22"
24"

3 RIGHT FRONT ARMHOLE

Next row (RS) Bind off 10 (12, 14, 14, 16) sts beginning of row, k to end—34 (32, 30, 30, 28) sts remain. (This number will be different if you altered length.)

Next row (WS) Yf, sl 1 p-wise, yb, k to end.

Row 1 (decrease row, RS) K1, SKP, k to end.

Row 2 Yf, sl 1 p-wise, yb, k to end.

Repeat these 2 rows until you have decreased 3 sts at the armhole and 31 (29, 27, 27, 25) sts remain. (This number will be different if you altered length.)

When you work the final decrease, mark this spot on the garment.

All following rows (unless otherwise directed) Yf, sl 1 p-wise, yb, k to end.

Work to 11 (12, 13, 14, 15)" from beginning, ending with WS row.

Where you see X____ on the photocopy, record the number of ridges you worked beyond the last decrease row.

Next row (RS) Yf, sl 1 p-wise, yb, k19 (17, 15, 15, 13) sts (this number will be different if you altered length), then bind off remaining 11 sts. Break yarn.

4 RIGHT BACK ARMHOLE

With WS facing, work as follows. With crochet hook and leaving tail to back, draw yarn through first st on left-hand needle. Work crochet cast-on until 16 sts cast on—36 (34, 32, 32, 30) sts on needle. (This number will be different if you altered length.)

All following rows (unless otherwise directed) Yf, sl 1 p-wise, yb, k to end.

Work to number of ridges recorded as X____ on your photocopy, ending with WS row.

The sl-st edge will not be worked at the beginning of some RS rows through the following shoulder and armhole shaping.

Row 1 (increase row, RS) K1, make 1 (M1, page 79), k to end.

Row 2 Yf, sl 1 p-wise, yb, k to end.

Repeat these 2 rows until you have increased 3 sts at the armhole and there are 39 (37, 35, 35, 33) sts on needle. (This number will be different if you altered length.)

With RS facing and with crochet hook, draw yarn through first st on left-hand needle. Work crochet cast-on until 10 (12, 14, 14, 16) sts cast on—49 sts now on needle.

Next row (RS) Yf, sl 1 p-wise, yb, k to end.

4,5
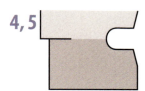

3

X____

1,2

A____

Small: 4 balls STYLECRAFT Fleece in color #3452

5 RIGHT BACK SHOULDER

Row 1 (increase row) (RS) K1, M1, k to end.
Rows 2 & 4 (WS) Yf, sl 1 p-wise, yb, k to end.
Row 3 (RS) K.
Repeat these last 4 rows, ending with row 2, until you have increased 4 sts at the shoulder and there are 53 sts on needle. (This number will be different if you altered length.)
Next row (RS) K to end.
Next row (WS) Yf, sl 1 p-wise, yb, k to end.
Repeat these last 2 rows 0 (1, 2, 3, 3) times more.
Place marker on fabric at beginning next RS row. (This marks beginning of back neck.)

6 CENTER BACK (ACROSS NECK)

All following rows (unless otherwise directed) Yf, sl 1 p-wise, yb, k to end.
Work to 7" from marker, ending with WS row. (Leave marker in place; you will need it when assembling.)
Place marker at beginning next RS row; you will need it when assembling.

7 LEFT BACK SHOULDER

The sl-st edge will not be worked at the beginning of some RS rows through the following shoulder and armhole shaping.
Next row (RS) K.
Next row (WS) Yf, sl 1 p-wise, yb, k to end.
Repeat these last 2 rows 0 (1, 2, 3, 3) times more.
Row 1 (decrease row, RS) K1, SKP, k to end.
Rows 2 & 4 (WS) Yf, sl 1 p-wise, yb, k to end.
Row 3 (RS) K.
Repeat these last 4 rows, ending with row 2, until you have decreased 4 sts at the shoulder and 49 sts remain. (This number will be different if you altered length.)

8 LEFT BACK ARMHOLE

Next row (RS) Bind off 10 (12, 14, 14, 16) sts beginning of row, k to end—39 (37, 35, 35, 33) sts remain. (This number will be different if you altered length.)
Next row (WS) Yf, sl 1 p-wise, yb, k to end.
Row 1 (decrease row, RS) K1, SKP, k to end.
Row 2 Yf, sl 1 p-wise, yb, k to end.

Repeat these 2 rows until you have decreased 3 sts at the armhole and 36 (34, 32, 32, 30) sts remain. (This number will be different if you altered length.)

All following rows (unless otherwise directed) Yf, sl 1 p-wise, yb, k to end.

Work to number of ridges recorded as X_____ on your photocopy, ending with WS row.

Next row (RS) Yf, sl 1 p-wise, yb, k19 (17, 15, 15, 13) sts (This number will be different if you altered length), then bind off remaining 16 sts. Break yarn.

9 LEFT FRONT ARMHOLE

With WS facing, work as follows. With crochet hook and leaving tail to back, draw yarn through first st on left-hand needle. Work crochet cast-on until 6 sts cast on—26 (24, 22, 22, 20) sts on needle. (This number will be different if you altered length.)

All following rows (unless otherwise directed) Yf, sl 1 p-wise, yb, k to end.

Work to number of ridges recorded as X_____ on your photocopy, ending with WS row.

The sl-st edge will not be worked at the beginning of some RS rows through the following shoulder and armhole shaping.

Row 1 (increase row, RS) K1, M1, k to end.
Row 2 Yf, sl 1 p-wise, yb, k to end.

Repeat these 2 rows until you have increased 3 sts at the armhole and there are 29 (27, 25, 25, 23) sts on needle. (This number will be different if you altered length.)

With RS facing and with crochet hook, draw yarn through first st on left-hand needle. Work crochet cast-on until 10 (12, 14, 14, 16) sts cast on—39 sts now on needle.

Next row (RS) Yf, sl 1 p-wise, yb, k to end.

10 LEFT FRONT SHOULDER

Row 1 (increase row, RS) K1, M1, k to end.
Rows 2 & 4 (WS) Yf, sl 1 p-wise, yb, k to end.
Row 3 (RS) K.

Repeat these last 4 rows, ending with row 2, until you have increased 4 sts at the shoulder and there are 43 sts on needle. (This number will be different if you altered length.)

Next row (RS) K.

Next row (WS) Yf, sl 1 p-wise, yb, k to end.

Repeat these last 2 rows 0 (1, 2, 3, 3) times more.

11 LEFT FRONT NECK

All following rows (unless otherwise directed) Yf, sl 1 p-wise, yb, k to end.
Continue until Left Front is same length as Right Front—11 (12, 13, 14, 15)" from side vent—ending with WS row.
Bind off.

FINISHING

Sew shoulder seams (ridges to ridges, page 42), leaving 7" (between markers) open at center back neck and 5½" open at each front neck. Sew buttons to Left Front to correspond to buttonholes.

9, 10, 11

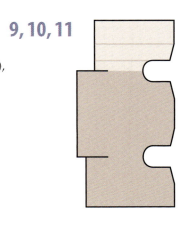

8

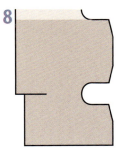

6, 7

In the side-to-side garments of this chapter, one front begins with a cast-on, and the other ends with a bind-off. There they sit, opposite each other along the front of the garment. How wonderful to have the option of making them match by opposing the bind-off with the crochet cast-on. But the crochet cast-on is not the easiest cast-on to master. If you can't, use another and save this one for later.

The crochet cast-on

This is the only cast-on that looks exactly like the bind-off. In fact, it is sometimes called the *bind-off cast-on.*

1 Make a slip knot, and put the slip knot onto a crochet hook (a slightly smaller size hook than the knitting needles you are using).

2 Hold hook in right hand, with yarn and knitting needle in left hand and with yarn under knitting needle. To give tension to yarn, wrap around index finger as shown.

3 To begin, anchor the tail by holding it in left hand and tight to left-hand needle.
4 Put crochet hook on top of left-hand needle.

Seaming in garter stitch

STITCHES TO STITCHES

In Chapter 1, you learned to seam ridges to ridges and then stitches to ridges. Here's the third possibility—stitches to stitches.

For clarity, seaming demonstrations are shown with contrasting-color yarn.

As you seam, pull your sewing yarn taut— just to resistance and not so you pucker your seam—every inch or so.

Do all of this with right side facing.
1 On edge of one piece to be seamed, take tapestry needle under first stitch, above bind-off edge.

2 Go across to other piece. Take tapestry needle under first stitch, below bind-off edge.

5 Take crochet hook to left of yarn …

6 …then behind yarn.

7 Draw yarn through loop on crochet hook. There is now a new stitch on left-hand needle.

8 Holding both needle and crochet hook in right-hand, take yarn to back, between crochet hook and knitting needle (above). Repeat Steps 4–8.

9 When your left-hand needle holds one stitch less than required for your cast-on, finish as follows: take yarn to back one more time, then transfer loop from crochet hook onto left-hand needle.

3 Go across to opposite piece. Take tapestry needle into place you came out of and under next stitch (above). Repeat Step 3.

Four stitches sewn, before pulling yarn taut

Stitches sewn, after pulling taut, with the bind-off edge into the seam allowance

Remember that *front* means the side of your knitting closest to you, and *back* means the side of your knitting away from you.

As you knit, note that when you are working a knit stitch, your yarn is to the back.

With yarn in front or back *yf yb*

Sometimes you are told to do something *with yarn in front.* This means that you are to bring the yarn between (not over) the left- and right-hand needles and to the front or back of your work.

WITH YARN IN FRONT, RIGHT-HAND CARRY

1 Take yarn toward the point of the right-hand needle...

2 ...then between the two needles...

3 ...so yarn sits in front of right-hand needle.

WITH YARN IN FRONT, LEFT-HAND CARRY

1 Take right-hand needle to right of yarn...

2 ...then behind yarn, so yarn sits in front of right-hand needle.

WITH YARN IN BACK

To take yarn to back, for either hold, move the yarn in the direction opposite that shown above.

Yarn over *yo*

To execute a *yarn over* means to put the yarn over the right-hand needle. This is a form of *increase* because, by taking the yarn over the needle, you have made a loop that can be used as a new stitch in the next row. It's a fairly holey form of increase and is most often used for buttonholes or in lacy patterns.

Oops! I forgot to make a yarn over. What do I do now? See page 150.

In a row of knit stitches, here is the easiest way to make a yarn over. Steps 1–2 show the right-hand carry, but the steps are the same for the left-hand carry.

1 Bring yarn to front.

2 Work next knit stitch but without taking yarn to back.

After knitting the next stitch, there will be an extra 'stitch' on your right-hand needle.

When you work the next row, this extra 'stitch' will be quite apparent.

KNITTING A YARN OVER

If you are instructed to knit through the front of the yarn over, just knit it as usual. The result will be quite holey.

If you are instructed to knit through the back of the yarn over, knit through the back side of the stitch. Doing so will close the hole.

In this chapter, yarn overs are used to make buttonholes. But the yarn of these garments is pretty thick, so these yarn overs will make pretty big holes. To tighten the buttonhole, you are instructed to knit through the back of the yarn overs.

A slip stitch *sl*

Sometimes patterns say to *slip* a stitch. This means you are to transfer a stitch from the left- to the right-hand needle without knitting it.

SLIPPING KNIT-WISE *k-wise*

1 Put right-hand needle into stitch as if to knit.

2 Slide stitch off left- and onto right-hand needle.

SLIPPING PURL-WISE *p-wise*

1 Put right-hand needle into stitch as if to purl, which is in the opposite direction from how you put it in as if to knit.

2 Slide stitch off left- and onto right-hand needle.

There are many wonderful people devoting time to the standardization of knitting terms.

But until this job is done, there are times when you simply will not be given enough information, and you will be told what to do and expected to know how to do it.

These rules regarding slip stitches help you sort this out . . . help you become a more intuitive knitter.

We slip stitches one way or another so that they are oriented properly when we next do something with them. You have just been told two different ways to do this. And patterns usually tell you which of these ways you are to slip a stitch. But sometimes they don't. Here are the rules for slipping stitches (if the directions don't say).

- If you are simply transferring the stitch from the left- to the right-hand needle—or onto a holder—and doing nothing else with it in this row, slip it purl-wise. This will orient it properly for when you work it later.
- If you are to slip the stitch and then do something with it in this row (like pass it over another stitch), slip it knit-wise. This will orient it properly for its next manipulation.

Slip 1, knit 1, pass slip stitch over *SKP*

This maneuver is a form of decreasing. The result is a decrease that slants to the left—as opposed to the knit-two-together decrease, which slants to the right. (These different slants will be more obvious in stitch patterns other than garter stitch.)

Oops! I forgot to work a decrease. What do I do now? See page 150.

1 Slip 1 knit-wise.

2 Knit 1 as usual.

3 Pass the slip stitch over the knit stitch, just like binding off.

4 An SKP, the result of a left-slanting decrease.

Make 1 *M1*

This maneuver is another form of increasing. The Make 1 is a little tighter and less visible than knitting into the front and back of a stitch.

1 With right-hand needle, lift yarn that lies between the two needles (above), and put the yarn onto the left-hand needle.

2 Knit through the back of it.

The result of a Make 1 increase

Oops! I forgot to work an increase. What do I do now? See page 150.

Measuring length

You can measure the length of your piece flat: this is how measurements are shown on the drawings. However, there are yarns that will stretch with the influence of gravity. Always double-check the measurement by holding the piece up and measuring it as it will be worn. If this measurement is significantly different from the one you get when measuring flat, the measurement as it will be worn is probably the one you want to pay attention to.

Once you have knit a piece (like the right sleeve) to the desired length, count the number of rows (or ridges) that it took to achieve this length. Then, when you knit a matching piece (like the left sleeve), you will work to this number of rows (or ridges).

It may seem like extra work—when matching two pieces of knitting—to count rows rather than just work to a measurement. But I don't trust a tape measure nearly as much as I do a row (or ridge) count! If you want your pieces to be exactly the same length, work to a row (or ridge) count.

As you become a more advanced knitter, you will learn other skills and stitch patterns, and you will leave behind this wonderful old friend, garter stitch. But I feel very fortunate to have had the opportunity to write this book and re-discover garter stitch (where we knit every stitch of every row).

One of it's most fabulous features is its stitch-to-row gauge:
1 stitch = 2 rows = 1 garter ridge. (If you get 12 stitches to 4", you will probably get 24 rows/12 garter ridges.) This may not mean all that much to you yet—especially if you haven't seen how other stitch patterns behave—but this simple, 1-to-1 ratio is both unusual and useful. This chapter explores this ratio, in pieces that are knit in more than one direction.

There is some pretty spectacular knitting—much more complex than this—whose core feature is this special relationship of stitches to rows. As you proceed on your knitting journey, be on the look out for it!

Chapter Four

The Patterns

Additional Skills

Small: 22 balls MUENCH Touch Me in color #3634

Women's M: 11 balls ISTEX Lopi in color #9118

EINSTEIN COAT

I love this coat … enough to have made two of them for myself! It is, truly, one of my favorite pieces of knitting. And it's not just me. The elegance of its construction seems to have universal appeal.

My friend, Heather, made herself one. She wore it while traveling, and a customs agent—not trained to be the most friendly person on the planet—gushed over it. This is a pretty momentous event in the life of a true beginner knitter—to have your work noticed, to have it admired, to be asked if you had knit it yourself, to be complimented on your knitting!

It's called the Einstein Coat because you feel like a genius when it's done: the fabric sits in your lap while you knit and turn the pieces as directed (without necessarily understanding why you do so) … and then you work two small seams … and voilá, a coat!

I also think this piece illustrates the elegant and simple aesthetic that Einstein thought to be a core feature of our universe.

After knitting the woman's version, it seemed to me that the guys and the kid ought to have their own. I don't know how the young boy felt about his garment, but the male model offered to buy his!

▌ *An adult coat may stretch 3" in length with wearing.*

Here's how!

There is a slip stitch at the edges of all garment pieces. This treatment makes the garment hang and assemble nicely. Failure to work these slip stitches will make the garment look sloppy. To learn it, to imbed it in your memory, I suggest you practice it in your gauge swatch.

So, here are special directions for your gauge swatch.
- *Cast on 15 stitches (sts). (Any cast-on is fine, but you could practice the crochet cast-on, page 74.)*
- *Work garter st with slip-stitch (sl-st) edge: with yarn in front (yf, page 76), slip first st purl-wise (sl 1 p-wise, page 78), take yarn to back (yb), k to end.*

- *Repeat this row to 13 garter ridges.*
- *Bind off.*
- *Piece should measure 4" x 4", without including sl sts, cast-on, or bind-off.*

1 LOWER BODY PIECE

With crochet cast-on and larger needle, cast on 29 (32, 38) sts for Child's,
44 sts for Man's,
56 sts for Woman's.
SHORTEN OR LENGTHEN HERE.
To shorten by 1", cast on 3 fewer sts. To lengthen by 1", cast on 3 more sts.
Work garter st with sl-st edge for 1 right-side (RS) row. Turn work. Hang marker to designate wrong side (WS). Move marker up piece as needed.
Continue garter st with sl-st edge, ending with WS row
to 100 (112, 136) ridges for Child's,
to 152 (164, 176, 188, 200) ridges for Adult's.
This is a large number of ridges, because it is an oversized garment and you're knitting the entire circumference. To make life easier, hang something—a piece of yarn, a paper clip—every 50 ridges, so you don't have to re-count.
The buttonholes are on the male side.

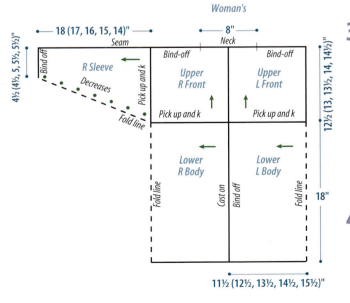

Woman's

18 (17, 16, 15, 14)" — 8" — Neck
Seam

4½ (4½, 5, 5½, 5½)"
Bind off

R Sleeve
Decreases
Fold line

Bind-off · Bind-off
Pick up and k · Pick up and k

Upper R Front · Upper L Front
Pick up and k · Pick up and k

Lower R Body · Lower L Body

Fold line · Cast on · Bind off · Fold line

12½ (13, 13½, 14, 14½)"
18"

11½ (12½, 13½, 14½, 15½)"

Begin buttonholes for Child's: *Next RS row* Yf, sl 1 p-wise, yb, k2 (2, 6), knit two together (k2tog, page 57), yarn over (yo, page 77), k8 (9, 8), k2tog, yo, k to end. Two buttonholes made.
Begin buttonholes for Adult's: *Next RS row* Yf, sl 1 p-wise, yb, k6, knit two together (k2tog, page 57), yarn over (yo, page 77), k12, k2tog, yo, k to end. Two buttonholes made.
End buttonholes for Both: *Next row* Working WS row as usual, k through back (B, page 77) of yo's (to tighten them).
Continue garter st with sl-st edge for 1 more ridge, ending with WS row.
Bind off.

2 UPPER RIGHT FRONT

With RS facing and larger needle, pick up and k 1 st in cast-on row of Lower Body Piece and then in the back of sl sts (page 98)
to 28 (31, 37) sts on needle for Child's,
to 41 (44, 47, 50, 53) sts on needle for Adult's.
Turn work.
Work garter st with sl-st edge, ending with WS row
to 21 (24, 30) ridges for Child's,
to 37 (38, 39, 40, 41) ridges for Adult's.
Bind off.

3 UPPER BACK

With RS facing and larger needle, and beginning in same sl st as last st of pick-up row for Upper Right Front, pick up and k 1 st in the back of sl sts
to 50 (56, 68) sts on needle for Child's,
to 76 (82, 88, 94, 100) sts on needle for Adult's.
Turn work.
Work garter st with sl-st edge, ending with WS row
to 21 (24, 30) ridges for Child's,
to 37 (38, 39, 40, 41) ridges for Adult's.
Bind off.

4 UPPER LEFT FRONT

With RS facing and larger needle, and beginning in same sl st as last st of pick-up row for Upper Back and ending in bind-off row of Lower Body Piece, pick up and k 1 st in the back of remaining sl sts

EXPERIENCE

- *very easy*
- *lots of knitting*
- *minimal finishing*

OVERSIZED FIT

Child's 2–4 (6–8, 10–12)
A 30 (34, 42)"
B 16 (18, 21½)"
C 19½ (22½, 27½)"

Adult's S (M, L, XL, XXL)
A 46 (50, 54, 58, 62)"
for adult's sizes
B 26½ (27, 27½, 28, 28½)"
for men's sizes
30½ (31, 31½, 32, 32½)"
for women's sizes
C 33" for men's sizes
29½" for women's sizes

10cm/4"

13 **GET GAUGE!**

13

- *over garter stitches and ridges*
- *with larger needles*
- *after blocking*

You'll need

1 2 3 4 **5** 6

- *bulky weight*
- *450 (550, 800) yds for children's sizes*
- *1100 (1200, 1300, 1400, 1500) yds for women's sizes*
- *men's sizes may take 50-100 yds less*
- *wool or wool blend*

- *1" buttons*
Four (four, five) for children's sizes, Six for adult's (without collar, one less)

I used

- *6mm/US 10*
- *5mm/US 8*

- *5–6mm/US H–G*

EINSTEIN COAT

to 28 (31, 37) sts on needle for Child's,
to 41 (44, 47, 50, 53) sts on needle for Adult's.
Turn work.
Work garter st with sl-st edge
to 5 (6, 2) ridges for Child's,
to 6 ridges for Adult's.
Begin buttonhole: *Next RS row* Yf, sl 1 p-wise, yb, k to
5 sts remaining, k2tog, yo, k3. One buttonhole made.
End buttonhole: *Next row* Working WS row as
usual, k through B of yo.
Continue garter st with sl-st edge
to 13 (15, 11) ridges from beginning for Child's,
to 19 ridges from beginning for Adult's.
Make buttonhole over next 2 rows as above.
Continue garter st with sl-st edge
to 21 (24, 20) ridges from beginning for Child's,
to 32 ridges from beginning for Adult's.
For Child's 2–4 (6–8) Bind off.
For all other sizes Make buttonhole over next 2
rows as above.
Continue garter st with sl-st edge
to 30 ridges from beginning for Child's 10–12,
to 37 (38, 39, 40, 41) ridges from beginning for Adult's.
Bind off.

5 RIGHT SLEEVE
With RS facing and larger needle, pick up and k 1 st
in bind-off row of Upper Right Front and then in the
back of every sl st down side of Upper Right Front
22 (25, 31) sts on needle for Child's,
38 (39, 40, 41, 42) sts on needle for Adult's.
Place marker to designate center of sleeve.
Working up side of Upper Back, pick up and k 1
st in the back of every sl st, ending in bind-off row
of Upper Back
44 (50, 62) sts on needle for Child's,
76 (78, 80, 82, 84) sts on needle for Adult's.
*Turn work.
Continue garter st with sl-st edge
to 6 ridges from beginning for Child's,
to 6 (3, 1, 1, 1) ridges from beginning for Adult's.
Next (decrease) row (RS) Work to 3 sts from center
marker, slip 1, knit 1, pass slip stitch over (SKP, page
79), k2, k2tog, k to end.
Work 3 more rows.
Repeat these last 4 rows, working decreases on
either side of center of sleeve each 4th row
to 24 sts remaining for Child's,
to 30 (30, 34, 36, 36) sts remaining OR to 16 (15,
14, 13, 12)" from beginning for Woman's (whichever
occurs first),

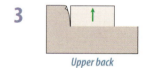
Left sleeve

Right sleeve

Upper left front

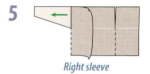
Upper back

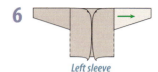
Upper right front

Lower body piece

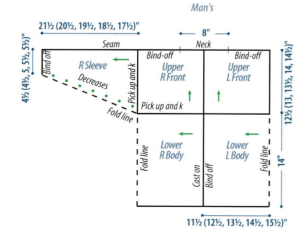

Man's

21½ (20½, 19½, 18½, 17½)"
8"
Seam
Neck
4½ (4½, 5, 5½, 5½)"
Bind off
R Sleeve
Decreases
Upper
R Front
Upper
L Front
Pick up and k
Fold line
Pick up and k
12½ (13, 13½, 14, 14½)"
Fold line
Lower
R Body
Lower
L Body
Fold line
Cast on
Bind off
14"
11½ (12½, 13½, 14½, 15½)"

Right, Man's L: 12 balls ISTEX
Lopi in color #9367
Child's 6–8: 5 balls ISTEX Lopi in
color #0085

EINSTEIN COAT

to 30 (30, 34, 36, 36) sts remaining OR to 19½ (18½, 17½, 16½, 15½)" from beginning for Man's (whichever occurs first).

For Adult's SHORTEN OR LENGTHEN HERE.

For Child's Continue garter st with sl-st edge to 10 (12, 15)" from beginning. SHORTEN OR LENGTHEN HERE. Change to smaller needles and continue sleeve to 12 (14, 17)". Bind off.

For Adult's If there are 30 (30, 34, 36, 36) sts remaining but sleeve is not yet required length, discontinue decreases, and work to length.

If sleeve is required length and there are more than this number of sts remaining, work 1 RS row as follows: Change to smaller needles and work across, decreasing sts evenly (page 99) to 30 (30, 34, 36, 36) sts.

On smaller needles, continue garter st with sl-st edge for 6 ridges.

Bind off.

6 LEFT SLEEVE

With RS facing and larger needle, pick up and k 1 st in bind-off row of Upper Back and then in the back of every sl st down the side of Upper Back

22 (25, 31) sts on needle for Child's,

38 (39, 40, 41, 42) sts on needle for Adult's.

Place marker to designate center of sleeve. Working up side of Upper Left Front, pick up and k 1 st in the back of every sl st, ending in bind-off row of Upper Left Front

44 (50 , 62) sts on needle for Child's,

76 (78, 80, 82, 84) sts on needle for Adult's.

Continue with directions for Right Sleeve from* to end.

FINISHING

If your yarn tears too easily, it is not appropriate for seaming. Use something stronger in a similar color. Tapestry yarn works well.

Beginning at Right Cuff, sew sl sts together (page 98) up Sleeve, then sew Right Front/Back bound-off sts together in same manner across Shoulder.

Leave 13 bound-off sts unsewn on Upper Right Front (for neck opening) for Child's;

leave 17 bound-off sts unsewn on Upper Right Front (for neck opening) for Adult's.

Reinforce stitching at end of seam (on WS) because there will be a lot of strain on the garment at this corner.

Beginning at Left Cuff, sew Left Sleeve and Shoulder in same manner. Sew buttons to Right Front to correspond to buttonholes.

Collar (for Woman's)

With RS facing and larger needle, and beginning at neck opening of Right Front, pick up and k 1 st in the back of remaining 17 bound-off sts along Right Front Neck. Pick up and k 1 st in corner—18 sts on needle. Pick up and k 1 st in the back of all bound-off sts along open Back Neck—46 to 48 sts on needle. Pick up and k 1 st in corner. Pick up and k 1 st in the back of remaining 17 bound-off sts along Left Front Neck—64 to 66 sts on needle.

Turn work.

Work garter st with sl-st edge to 2 ridges from beginning.

Begin buttonhole: *Next row* (RS) Yf, sl 1 p-wise, yb, k to 5 sts remaining, k2tog, yo, k3.

End buttonhole: *Next row* Working WS row as usual, k through back of yo. Continue garter st with sl-st edge to 11 ridges from beginning.

Bind off.

Left, Women's M: 11 balls ISTEX Lopi in color #9718

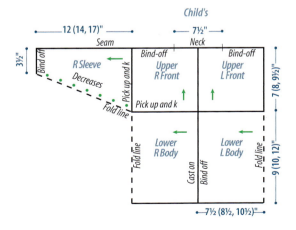

7 balls: LANG Kyoto in color #004

YOUR BASIC BAG

The coats that precede and the coats that follow are, admittedly, an awful lot of knitting … although I think they're worth the effort. But to introduce knitting in all directions without all this work, I offer a bag.

Final measurements are approximate (see drawing) because different ribbons will hang—and stretch with wear—differently. Good thing that gauge really doesn't matter here!

Here's how!

Even though gauge is offered as a range, you need to do a gauge swatch to determine needle size. Use needles that will make your fabric firm— probably 1–2 sizes smaller than recommended on the yarn label.

STRAP

1 With your preferred cast-on (I used the crochet cast-on, page 74), cast on 14 stitches (sts).
With yarn in front (yf, page 76), slip first st purl-wise (sl 1 p-wise, page 78), take yarn to back (yb), k all sts. Turn work.

It is really important to slip the first st of every row. Failure to do so will make the strap look sloppy.
Repeat this row to 74". This length will give a doubled Strap of 17".

This strap length is adjustable; if you wish, you may make the strap longer in the finishing.
Bind off.

EXPERIENCE
• easy
• simple finishing

10cm/4"
15-19
17-21
• over garter stitches and ridges

You'll need
1 2 3 **4** 5 6
• medium weight
• 525 yds
• soft ribbon

• one 2" decorative button or toggle
• approximately ½yd (40–60" wide) lining fabric
• 2yds of strong yarn (for seaming, if ribbon tears too easily)

I used
• 4mm/US 6

• 4mm/US F

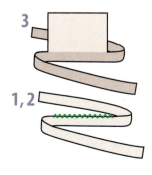

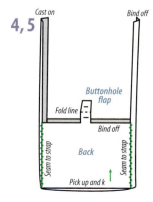

FRONT

2 Fold Strap in half to find center at bottom. Measure 7" to right of center; place marker. Measure 14" to left of marker (7" past center); place marker. Pick up 1 st in each garter ridge just below sl-st edge of Strap (page 98); this is now the wrong side (WS) of Strap. Record the number of stitches you picked up. With right side (RS) facing, k all sts on needle.

3 Continue to knit all sts to 13" from beginning, ending with WS row.
Bind off.

BACK

On WS of strap, find ridge at beginning and then at end of pick-up row for purse Front. Cross to other edge of strap (still on WS), and place markers corresponding to these ridges. With WS facing, pick up 1 st in each garter ridge between markers below sl-st edge. (The result should be the same number of stitches that you picked up for the purse Front.). Work as from* to end of Front, but do not bind off at 13".

4 Buttonhole flap

Next row (RS) Bind off to center 14 sts, k14, bind off remaining sts. Cut yarn.
Return to 14 sts on needle, ready to work WS row. Attach yarn.
Row 1 Yf, sl 1 p-wise, yb, k to end.
Repeat this row to 14 ridges, ending with WS row.
Next row (front of buttonhole) Yf, sl 1 p-wise, k4, make one-row buttonhole (page 96), binding off 4 sts in center of row, then finish row.
Continue as Row 1 (above) to 18 ridges from beginning, ending with WS row.
Next row (RS) Bind off and draw yarn through last stitch, but do not cut yarn.
Turn work so WS of Buttonhole flap is facing.
Pick up and k 14 sts along Front (closest) edge of bind-off. Work as Row 1 (above) to 4 ridges.
Next row (back of buttonhole) Yf, sl 1 p-wise, yb, k4, make one-row buttonhole, binding off 4 sts in center of row, then finish row.
Continue as Row 1 (above) to 18 ridges.
Bind off.

5 FINISHING

Using strong yarn, sew sides of purse Front and Back to just inside WS of Strap (ridges to ridges, page 42). Sew front and back of Buttonhole flap together at sides. Sew bind-off edge of Buttonhole flap to inside of Purse Back.
Sew buttonhole together at edges, if needed.
Overlap Strap and temporarily attach cast-on edge to top of purse at one side and bound-off edge to top of purse at other side. If you like the strap at this length, proceed with seaming instructions.
If you want a longer Strap, wet it and stretch it to the length you want. (Consider that it will stretch a little more with wear.) Let dry.
With Strap overlapping along entire length (for stability), finish Strap as follows:
Attach bound-off edge of Strap to RS, where it emerges from other side of purse.
Attach cast-on edge of Strap to WS, where it emerges from other side of purse.
Attach Straps together along length.
Wash purse (to set size before cutting lining).

LINING

If you use this purse without a lining, it will stretch a great deal and might tear along the seam lines.

Measure width of purse. Cut lining to this width + 1" (for ½" seam allowances). Measure height of purse. Cut lining to twice this measurement + 1" (for ½" hem allowance).
With RS together, fold lining in half (along width), and sew side seams with ½" seam allowance.
Turn ½" hem to WS around top edge, and sew ¼" from edge.
Insert lining into purse, WS of lining to WS of purse.
Sew top edge of lining to inside top edge of purse.
Sew on button to correspond to buttonhole, sewing through lining to secure.

7 balls LANG Kyoto in color #98

NOT-SO-WARM COAT

Noticing how often I wore the Einstein Coat prompted me to think about other versions. What about lighter-weight yarns for warmer weather or dressier occasions? Two garments are shown here. The first (in chocolate) is in a lovely rayon blend. The second (in blue, page 80) is in the yummiest yarn—but one that requires special instructions. (See all the notes for Touch Me yarn throughout the pattern.)

The yarns I used are luscious but heavy. So the measurements as knit are different from the measurements as worn, because heavier yarns will hang to a slimmer silhouette (2" slimmer) and will stretch in length (up to 6").

The A, B, C measurements are for the garment as worn (and a range of lengths is given).

Measurements on the drawing are for the garment as knit (The shorter length on the Lower Body piece is for Touch Me only. I made it shorter because this yarn is so dear!)

If you make this garment in a less heavy yarn (see orange one, page 93), the measurements as worn will be the same as the measurements as knit, and your garment will be oversized rather than loose fit.

Size M: 12 balls PATON'S Katrina in color #10031

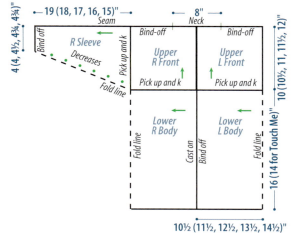

EXPERIENCE
- *very easy*
- *lots of knitting*
- *minimal finishing*

LOOSE FIT

S (M, L, XL, XXL)
Measurements as worn
A 40 (44, 48, 52, 56)"
B 31–34"
C 29"

10cm/4"
18 GET GAUGE!
18
- *over garter stitches and ridges*
- *after washing and drying Touch Me*

You'll need
1 2 3 **4** 5 6
- *medium weight*
- *1850 (1960, 2120, 2300, 2460) yds*
- *For Touch Me only, 1350 (1430, 1540, 1650, 1740) yds*
- *something luscious*

- *Six ¾" buttons*

I used
- *4mm/US 6*
- *3.5mm/US 4*

- *4–5mm/US F–H*

Special note for Touch Me:
As you knit occasional loops (called 'worms') may appear . . . from nowhere and when you weren't looking! Don't fret. They disappear when you wash the piece as directed.

Here's how!

There is a slip stitch at the edges of all garment pieces. This treatment makes the garment hang and assemble nicely. Failure to work these slip stitches will make the garment look sloppy. To learn it, to imbed it in your memory, I suggest you practice it in your gauge swatch.

So, here are special directions for your gauge swatch
• Cast on 20 stitches (sts). (Any cast-on is fine, but you could practice the crochet cast-on, page 74.)
• Work garter st with slip-stitch edge: with yarn in front (yf, page 76), slip first st purl-wise (sl 1 p-wise, page 78), take yarn to back (yb), k to end.
• Repeat this row to 18 garter ridges.
• Bind off.
• Piece should measure 4" x 4", without including sl sts, cast-on, or bind-off.
• Touch Me will measure 4½" x 4½", without including slip sts, cast-on row, or bind-off row. Wash swatch as directed below, then re-measure. Final measurement should be 4" x 4".

Washing instructions for Touch Me:
Despite what the yarn label says, wash and rinse in warm water and in the washing machine. It will come out of the washer small and hard. Dry in a warm dryer, and it will soften to something extraordinarily beautiful.

1 LOWER BODY PIECE

With crochet cast-on and larger needle, cast on 72 sts. *For Touch Me only*, cast on 56 sts. SHORTEN OR LENGTHEN HERE.

To shorten by 1", cast on 4 fewer stitches. To lengthen by 1", cast on 4 more stitches.

Work garter st with sl-st edge for 1 right-side (RS) row. Turn work. Hang marker to designate wrong side (WS). Move marker up piece as needed.
Work to 3 ridges from beginning, ending with WS row.
Begin buttonholes: *Next row (RS)* Yf, sl 1 p-wise, yb, knit two together (k2tog, page 57), yarn over

(yo, page 77), *k10, k2tog, yo, repeat from * once more, k to end. Three buttonholes made.
End buttonholes: *Next row* Working WS row as usual, k through back (B, page 77) of yo's (to tighten them). Work in garter st with sl-st edge to 191 (210, 226, 245, 264) ridges from beginning, ending with WS row.

This is a large number of ridges, because it is an oversized garment and you're knitting the entire circumference. To make life easier, hang something—a piece of yarn, a paper clip—every 50 ridges, so you don't have to re-count.
Bind off.

2 UPPER RIGHT FRONT

With RS facing and larger needle, pick up and k 1 st in cast-on row of Lower Body Piece and then in the back of sl sts (page 98) to 50 (55, 59, 64, 69) sts on needle.
Turn work.
Work garter st with sl-st edge for entire piece.
At 11 ridges from beginning, work as follows.
Begin buttonhole: *Next row (RS)* Yf, sl 1 p-wise, yb, k2, yo, k2tog, k to end. One buttonhole made.
End buttonhole: *Next row* Working WS row as usual, k through B of yo.
Continue to 21 ridges from beginning.
Make buttonhole over next 2 rows as above.
Continue to 32 ridges from beginning.
Make buttonholes over next 2 rows as above.
Continue to 44 (47, 50, 52, 54) ridges from beginning, ending with WS row.
For Touch Me only, work to 41 (44, 47, 49, 51) ridges from beginning.
Bind off.

3 UPPER BACK

With RS facing and larger needle, and beginning in same sl st as last st of pick-up row for Upper Right Front, pick up and k 1 st in the back of sl sts to 95 (104, 112, 121, 130) sts on needle.
Turn work.
Work garter st with sl-st edge to 44 (47, 50, 52, 54) ridges from beginning, ending with WS row.
For Touch Me only, work to 41 (44, 47, 49, 51) ridges from beginning.
Bind off.

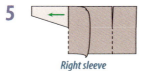

6   Left sleeve

5   Right sleeve

4   Upper left front

3   Upper back

2   Upper right front

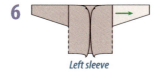

1   Lower body piece

NOT-SO-WARM COATS

4 UPPER LEFT FRONT

With RS facing and larger needle, and beginning in same sl st as last st of pick-up row for Upper Back and ending in bind-off row of Lower Body Piece, pick up and k 1 st in the back of remaining sl sts— 50 (55, 59, 64, 69) sts on needle.
Turn work.
Work garter st with sl-st edge to 44 (47, 50, 52, 54) ridges from beginning, ending with WS row.
For Touch Me only, work to 41 (44, 47, 49, 51) ridges.
Bind off.

5 RIGHT SLEEVE

With RS facing and larger needle, pick up and k 1 st in bind-off row of Upper Right Front and then in the back of every sl st down side of Upper Right Front— 45 (48, 51, 53, 55) sts on needle.
For Touch Me only—42 (45, 48, 50, 52) sts on needle.
Place marker to designate center of sleeve. Working up side of Upper Back, pick up and k 1 st in the back of every sl st, ending in bind-off row of Upper Back— 90 (96, 102, 106, 110) sts on needle.
For Touch Me only— 84 (90, 96, 100, 104) sts on needle.
*Turn work.
Work garter st with sl-st edge to 12 (8, 6, 4, 2) ridges from beginning.
Next (decrease) row (RS) Work to 3 sts from center marker, slip 1, knit 1, pass slip stitch over (SKP, page 79), k2, k2tog, k to end.
Work garter st with sl-st edge for 3 more rows.
Repeat these last 4 rows, working decreases on either side of center of sleeve each 4th row to 40 (40, 42, 44, 44) sts remaining OR to 17½ (16½, 15½, 14½, 13½)" from beginning (whichever occurs first). SHORTEN OR LENGTHEN HERE. If there are 40 (40, 42, 44, 44) sts remaining but sleeve is not yet required length, discontinue decreases, and work to length. If sleeve is required length and there are more than 40 (40, 42, 44, 44) sts remaining, work 1 row as follows: Change to smaller needles and work across, decreasing sts evenly (page 99) to 40 (40, 42, 44, 44) sts. On smaller needles, continue garter st with sl-st edge for 1½". Bind off.

6 LEFT SLEEVE

With RS facing and larger needle, pick up and k 1 st in bind-off row of Upper Back and then in the back of every sl st down side of Upper Back— 45 (48, 51, 53, 55) sts on needle.
For Touch Me only— to 42 (45, 48, 50, 52) sts on needle.
Place marker to designate center of sleeve.
Working up side of Upper Left Front, pick up and k 1 st in the back of every sl st, ending in bind-off row of Upper Left Front—90 (96, 102, 106, 110) sts on needle.
For Touch Me only— to 84 (90, 96, 100, 104) sts on needle.
Continue with directions for Right Sleeve from* to end.

FINISHING

Beginning at Right Cuff, sew sl sts together (page 98) up Sleeve, then sew Right Front/Back bound-off sts together in same manner across Shoulder until 21 bound-off sts remain un-sewn on Upper Right Front (for neck opening).

> *Reinforce stitching at end of seam (on WS) because there will be a lot of strain on the garment at this corner.*

Beginning at Left Cuff, sew Left Sleeve and Shoulder in same manner.
Sew buttons to Left Front to correspond to buttonholes.
For Touch Me only, wash and dry as directed in notes on gauge swatch. Tails may come loose with washing and need to be re-secured.

EXPERIENCE

- *very easy*
- *minimal finishing*

OVERSIZED FIT

0–3 (6–9, 12) months for coat

A 20 (22, 25)"
B 10½ (11½, 13)"
C 11 (13, 15¼)"

0–3 for bunting

A 19"
B 14½" (to crotch)
C 11"

10cm/4"

20   GET CLOSE
20

- *over garter stitches and ridges*

You'll need

1 2 **3** 4 5 6

- *light weight*
- *something soft*

FOR COAT
330 (420, 550) yds
optional:
105 yds for hood

FOR BUNTING
210 yds in chartreuse (C1)
210 yds in periwinkle (C2) (includes 105 yds for hood)
105 yds in mustard (C3)
105 yds in tangerine (C4)

- *Five ¾" buttons, coat*
- *Eight ⅝" buttons, bunting*

I used

- *3.75mm/US 5*

- *3.5–4mm/US E–F*

Coat, 0–3 months: 3 balls SANDNES Smart in color #5226
Bunting: 6 balls Light-weight yarn

BABY ALBERT COAT & BUNTING

Is it stereotyping to suggest knitting for a baby? I suppose so. But it's a wonderful thing to knit for a baby—we get to make something precious for someone precious, and we get to practice our skills on something really small.

My first version of the Einstein Coat was actually knit in a newborn size—a tiny little mock up to see if it worked. But the heavier yarn was not soft enough for a baby, so this lighter-weight coat evolved.

I finished the baby coat and thought, "How cute is that?! Where can we go from here?" The result is this bunting. Isn't it great to see babies in really bright colors?

Only one size is offered for the bunting because larger sizes would require shaping to accommodate a diaper and I didn't want to complicate this easy pattern.

Here's how!

There is a slip stitch at the edges of all garment pieces. This treatment makes the garment hang and assemble nicely. Failure to work these slip stitches will make the garment look sloppy. To learn it, to imbed it in your memory, I suggest you practice it in your gauge swatch.
So, here are special directions for your gauge swatch.

- *Cast on 22 stitches (sts). (Any cast-on is fine, but you could practice the crochet cast-on, page 74.)*
- *Work garter st with slip-stitch (sl-st) edge: with yarn in front (yf, page 76), slip first st purl-wise (sl 1 p-wise, page 78), take yarn to back (yb), k to end.*
- *Repeat this row to 20 garter ridges.*
- *Bind off.*
- *Piece should measure 4" x 4", without including sl sts, cast-on, or bind-off.*

1 LOWER BODY PIECE

With crochet cast-on, cast on
27 (30, 35) sts for Coat,
48 sts in C1 for Bunting.
The C1, C2, C3, and C4 refer to the colors used. Use the yarn list and the photo as your guide.

BABY ALBERT COAT & BUNTING

Work garter st with sl-st edge
to 99 (107, 123) ridges from beginning for Coat,
to 95 ridges from beginning for Bunting.

This is a large number of ridges. To make life easier, hang something—a piece of yarn, a paper clip—every 20 ridges, so you don't have to re-count. Buttonholes are on the male side.

Begin buttonholes: *Next row* (RS) Yf, sl 1 p-wise, yb, k5, knit two together (k2tog, page 57), yarn over (yo, page 77), k7, k2tog, yo, k to end. Two buttonholes made.

End buttonholes: *Next row* Working as usual, k through back (B, page 77) of yo's (to tighten them). Continue with garter st with sl-st edge for 2 more ridges. Bind off.

2 UPPER RIGHT FRONT
With RS facing, pick up and k 1 st in cast-on row of Lower Body Piece and then in the back of sl sts (page 98)
to 27 (29, 33) sts on needle for Coat,
with C3 and to 27 sts on needle for Bunting.
Turn work.
Work garter st with sl-st edge, ending with WS row
to 23 (26, 29) ridges for Coat,
to 23 ridges for Bunting.
Bind off.

3 UPPER BACK
With RS facing, and beginning in same sl st as last st of pick-up row for Upper Right Front, pick up and k 1 st in the back of sl sts
to 52 (56, 64) sts on needle for Coat,
with C3 and to 48 sts on needle for Bunting.
Turn work.
Work garter st with sl-st edge, ending with WS row:
to 23 (26, 29) ridges for Coat,
to 23 ridges for Bunting.
Bind off.

4 UPPER LEFT FRONT
With RS facing, beginning in same sl st as last st of pick-up row for Upper Back and ending in bind-off row of Lower Body Piece, pick up and k 1 st in the back of remaining sl sts
to 27 (29, 33) sts on needle for Coat,
with C3 and to 27 sts on needle for Bunting.

Turn work.
Work garter st with sl-st edge for entire piece.
At 2 ridges from beginning, work as follows.

Begin buttonhole: *Next row* (RS) Yf, sl 1 p-wise, yb, k to 5 sts remaining, k2tog, yo, k to end. 1 buttonhole made.

End buttonhole: *Next row* Working WS row as usual, k through B of yo.
Continue to 10 ridges from beginning.
Make buttonhole over next 2 rows as above.
Continue to 18 ridges from beginning.
Make buttonholes over next 2 rows as above.
Continue as follows:
to 23 (26, 29) ridges for Coat,
to 23 ridges for Bunting.
Bind off.

5 RIGHT SLEEVE
With RS facing, pick up and k 1 st in bind-off row of Upper Right Front and in the back of every sl st down side of Upper Right Front to 24 (27, 30) sts on needle for Coat, with C4 and to 24 sts on needle for Bunting.
Place marker to designate center of sleeve. Working up side of Upper Back, pick up and k 1 st in the back of every sl st, ending in bind-off row of Upper Back to 48 (54, 60) sts on needle for Coat, to 48 sts on needle for Bunting.
*Turn work.
Work garter st with sl-st edge to 6 (6, 12) ridges for Coat and 6 ridges for Bunting.

Next (decrease) row (RS) Work to 3 sts from center marker, slip 1, knit 1, pass slip stitch over (SKP, page 79), k2, k2tog, k to end.
Work 3 (5, 5) more rows for Coat, 3 more rows for Bunting.
Continue, working decreases on either side of center of sleeve each 4 or 6 rows (as directed above)

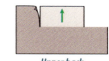
3 Upper back

2 Upper right front

1 Lower body piece

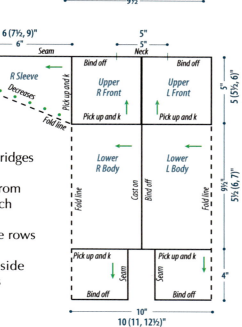

to 30 (36, 40) sts remaining for Coat,
to 30 sts remaining for Bunting.
Continue without decreases to 6 (7½, 9)" from beginning for Coat, 6" for Bunting.
Bind off.

LEFT SLEEVE

With RS facing, pick up and k 1 st in bind-off row of Upper Back and then in the back of every sl st down side of Upper Back
to 24 (27, 30) sts on needle for Coat,
with C2 and to 24 sts on needle for Bunting.
Place marker to designate center of sleeve. Working up side of Upper Left Front, pick up and k 1 st in the back of every sl st, ending in bind-off row of Upper Left Front
to 48 (54, 60) sts on needle for coat,
to 48 sts on needle for Bunting.
Continue with directions for Right Sleeve from* to end.

FINISHING

Beginning at Right Cuff, sew sl sts together (page 98) up Sleeve, then sew Right Front/Back bound-off sts together in same manner across Shoulder until 13 bound-off sts remain un-sewn on Upper Right Front (for neck opening).

Reinforce stitching at end of seam (on WS) because there will be a lot of strain on the garment at this corner.

Beginning at Left Cuff, sew Left Sleeve and Shoulder in same manner.
Sew buttons to Right Front to correspond to buttonholes.

7 LEFT LEG (BUNTING ONLY)

Make this piece in C4.
Hold garment upside down, ready to pick up sts along bottom edge of Lower Body Piece.
With RS facing, skip bind-off row plus 6 ridges along edge of Left Front (side with Buttonholes), then pick up and k 1 st in the back of sl sts to 40 sts on needle.
Turn work.
Work garter st with sl-st edge to 19 ridges.
Bind off.

8 RIGHT LEG (BUNTING ONLY)

Make this piece in C2.
Return to Back of garment, ready to pick up sts along bottom edge of Lower Body Piece.
With RS facing, skip 6 stitches adjacent to the Left Leg, then pick up and k 1 st in the back of sl sts to 40 sts on needle.
Turn work.
Work garter st with sl-st edge to 19 ridges.
Bind off.
Beginning at bottom of Right Leg, sew sl sts together up right inseam. Lap buttonhole edge over what will become the button edge, and sew sl sts together across crotch, then sew sl sts together down left inseam.

9 HOOD (BUNTING ONLY)

Make this piece in C2.
With RS facing, skip sl-st edge and first bound-off st of button edge, then pick up and k 1 st in the back of every bound-off st along Right Front Neck—12 sts on needle. Pick up and k 1 st in corner, then pick up and k 1 st in the back of all bound-off sts across Back Neck—35 sts on needle. Pick up and k 1 st in corner, then pick up and k 1 st in the back of every bound-off st along Left Front Neck, leaving last bound-off st plus sl-st edge unused—48 sts on needle.
Work garter st with sl-st edge to 3 ridges.
Next (increase) row (RS) Yf, sl 1 p-wise, yb, *k1, knit in front and back of next stitch (kf&b, page 57), repeat from*, k1—71 sts on needle.
Work garter st with sl-st edge to 31 ridges from beginning.
Bind off.
Fold hood in half, with fold-line at center back.
Working from front of hood to back, sew bound-off edges together.
Optional To form bag, sew bound-off edges together at bottom of legs.

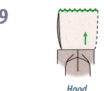
9
Hood

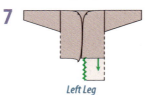
8
Right leg

7
Left Leg

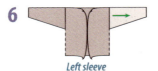
6

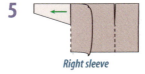
5
Left sleeve

Right sleeve

4
Upper left front

The garments of this chapter do not begin with the cable cast-on. They begin with the crochet cast-on, so that all edges of the pieces look the same.

But the cable cast-on is given here because it is used for the one-row buttonhole of the purse pattern.

Whether or not you make this purse, and whether or not you use this particular buttonhole, you should always use the cable cast-on when you need to cast on for a buttonhole. It's also a great cast-on for ribbing . . . once you learn ribbing!

The cable cast-on

Here's a cast-on that is neat, firm, and pretty.

1 Start with a slip knot on left-hand needle. Put right-hand needle into slip knot as if to knit . . .

2 . . . then draw through loop (above), and place loop back onto left-hand needle. (So far, this is identical to the knitted cast-on, page 18.)

3 For the next and all following stitches, instead of putting right-hand needle into the first stitch on the left-hand needle, put it between this stitch and the next stitch.

The one-row buttonhole

Here is the best choice for a sizable buttonhole.

1 With right side facing, work to where you want your buttonhole.
Bring yarn forward and slip one stitch purl-wise.

2 Take yarn to back. (Leave yarn to back; you won't need it until Step 8.)

3 Slip next stitch, purl-wise, from left-hand needle onto right-hand needle.

4 Pass the previously slipped stitch over the one just slipped (above): one stitch is bound off.
Repeat Steps 3–4 until you have the required number of stitches bound off.

7 Turn work. Take yarn to back.

8 Using cable cast-on (above), cast on one less than the number of stitches you bound off . . .

9 . . . draw through the loop for the last cast-on stitch, as usual, but just before putting this loop onto left-hand needle . . .

10 . . . bring the working yarn through to the front, between the two needles.

4 Draw through a loop as usual …

5 ..then place loop back onto left-hand needle (above).
Repeat Steps 3–5 until all stitches are cast on.

Five stitches cast on, and the start of a sixth

5 One stitch remains on right-hand needle.

6 Slip this remaining stitch back to the left-hand needle.

If you simply cast on the number of stitches for the buttonhole, without the maneuver done to the last stitch in the one-row buttonhole in Steps 9–11, you will produce a dreadful loop that will interfere with your buttonhole.

Whichever buttonhole you make, if it involves binding off and then casting on, use this trick, to bring the yarn forward with the final cast-on and avoid a loop that will interfere with your buttonhole.

11 Now put the last cast-on stitch onto left-hand needle (above).
12 Turn work, and continue with row as usual.

A completed buttonhole, right side facing

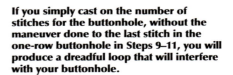

Picking up and knitting in the back of a slip-stitch edge

A slip-stitch edge looks just like the crochet cast-on and the bind-off. To pick up and knit from the back of this edge, follow Steps 1–3.

1 Do all of this with right side facing.
Put right-hand needle into back edge of first slip stitch. (This appears right at the cast-on or bound-off edge.)

2 Draw working yarn through, to form a stitch (above).

3 Put right-hand needle into back edge of next slip stitch (as in Step 1) and draw yarn through to form a stitch. Repeat Step 3.

Three stitches picked up and knit, plus the start of a fourth

Picking up below a slip-stitch edge

This is very similar to picking up from garter ridges (page 41), except that those ridges were on the edge of a piece, and these are not.

1 Do all of this with wrong side facing.
Put left-hand needle, from left to right, through each garter ridge that sits just next to the slip stitch.

An entire row picked-up

The right side, after a few rows of knitting

Seaming a slip-stitch edge

1 Do all this with right side facing.
Take tapestry needle under outside edge of first slip stitch.

2 Go across to opposite piece. Take tapestry needle into outside edge of first slip stitch, then come up to the front through outside edge of next slip stitch.

3 Go across to opposite piece. Take tapestry needle into place you came out of, then come back up through outside edge of next slip stitch. Repeat Step 3.

Decreasing evenly

When patterns tell you to decrease evenly, they mean to spread decreases evenly across one row.

1. You need two numbers: the number of sts you start with and the number of sts to decrease. *For example, you start with 36 and are to decrease to 30, so you are to decrease 6.*

2. Divide the number of sts you start with by the number of sts to decrease. *36 ÷ 6 = 6 = The Result.*

3. To decrease evenly across the row, *work 2 less than The Result, make a decrease, repeat from*.
   *In this example, *work 4, k2tog or SKP, repeat from*.*
   If The Result is not a whole number, do exactly as in Step 3, then work the remaining sts at the end of the row.

Increasing evenly

When patterns tell you to increase evenly, they mean to spread increases evenly across one row.

1. You need two numbers: the number of sts you start with and the number of sts to increase.
   For example, you start with 30 and are to increase to 36, so you are to increase 6.

2. Divide the number of sts you start with by the number of sts to increase. *30 ÷ 6 = 5 = The Result.*

3. To increase evenly across the row, *work 1 less than The Result, make an increase in the next st, repeat from*.
   *In this example, *work 4, kf&b, repeat from*.*

4. Or, to increase evenly across the row, *work to The Result, make an increase in the space between, repeat from*.
   *In this example, *work 5, M1, repeat from*.*
   If The Result is not a whole number, do exactly as in Steps 3 or 4, then work the remaining sts at the end of the row.

For clarity, seaming is shown in contrasting-color yarn.

As you seam, pull your sewing yarn taut— just to resistance and not so you pucker your seam—every inch or so.

Four stitches sewn, before pulling taut

The finished seam, after pulling taut

DEVELOPING AN AESTHETIC

It's easy enough to assume that beginner projects, in any domain, will be dull, simplistic, even crudely fashioned. But who's going to love our craft if this is what we produce? And is this how it has to be?

Einstein is reported to have said that if it is *beautiful* then it must be true. I think he meant that the universe has an underlying order that is both elegant and simple. It's not the only aesthetic that works, but it's the aesthetic to which this book is dedicated.

As I worked through the designs for this book—trying for easy pieces you would really want to knit and wear, trying for a variety that would speak to all ages, styles, sizes, climates, price ranges— there were some surprising discoveries:
- how much I loved knitting such simple pieces;
- how the pieces of this book are the ones I choose to wear;
- how incredibly positive advanced knitters have been about the styles in this book.

I am one of those advanced knitters, but I don't know that I have any ambition to do complex knitting again!

Because the knitting in this book is so simple, it's always fashionable, always easy to find something to wear it with, and I find myself building a wardrobe around what I have made as I never did before. (One cool, Canadian spring day, I was wearing five pieces at once: a coat from Chapter 4, a scarf from Chapter 1, a purse from Chapter 4, a sweater from Chapter 6, and socks from Book 2. It made me smile.)

As you become a more advanced knitter, you'll have an opportunity to run your personal aesthetic through your fingers and into your work. Whatever aesthetic you bring to life, I hope you discover as much joy in the experience as I have.

As you may have seen already, all yarn is not wool. There are other fabulous fibers and textures available. But still, somehow, the predominant assumption is that knitting involves wool. Yarn shops are even sometimes referred to as wool shops.

Well, there are places and times that, as wonderful as it is, we don't want to wear wool: the most obvious of these would be the summer. In warmer weather, we turn to cotton.

Cotton's great for summer because it transfers heat away from the body. But cotton doesn't always translate into the wonderful summer sweaters we'd expect 'cause it's heavy . . . and heavy can be warm.

For a garment to be cool, it has to be made in a yarn that is both cool and light. Given cotton's weight, this isn't always easy (although there are cotton blends that are light, and I use one in the child's garment that follows). But there are ways to produce light fabric from heavy yarn, and that's what the pieces in this chapter are all about—light, airy, sheer fabric.

There are opaque areas in these garments, balancing the sheer and covering the body where it needs to be covered. It was my challenge to figure out how to make this all happen, without sacrificing modesty and while keeping the patterns relatively easy.

One feature of these garments that will make them less easy for a beginner is the very fact that they are knit in cotton. This fiber is heavy and it has little elasticity. This lack of elasticity might make getting gauge a challenge. Be prepared to make swatches on ever-smaller needles until you match gauge. And while its heaviness is exactly what's needed to hold the garment's shape, the fabric will stretch. Measure your length frequently, with the garment held up, not lying flat, and read about Washing Cotton (page 21).

CHAPTER FIVE

The Patterns

Additional Skills

Woman's M: 13 skeins, BERROCO Linet in color #3318

SALLY'S FAVORITE SUMMER SWEATER

I first knit this sweater while sailing in the Great Lakes. When finished, I only had one little mirror in our stateroom to examine the result, but it looked fabulous! It's now my summer standby garment, 'cause it's light and cool … and it hides all sins!

If you are like me, you'll want more than one: a first in a neutral color that goes with everything, then a second in a color that looks fabulous on you! (I now have a third, and am contemplating a fourth—might that be excessive?)

A word about the sizing. This piece may seem wide, but there are three reasons for this. The first is that it's meant to be a fun, oversized piece. The second is that it's for warm weather, and I find garments that hang free from the body much cooler to wear. And the third is that is has to clear the hips and so may demand more ease than a garment that only has to clear the bust.

To choose a size, measure your bust and hips. Add 6" to whichever is larger. This measurement, or the next size larger, is the appropriate size. Don't worry if it seems wide: the line at the shoulders will be slimming.

Here is how the Sheer and Opaque fabrics are produced. It's easy to remember, and putting it up front makes the pattern easier to read.

SHEER FABRIC
Right-side (RS) rows Knit (k) all stitches (sts) onto smaller needle.
Wrong-side (WS) rows K all sts onto larger needle.
OPAQUE FABRIC
All rows K all sts with smaller needle(s).

Here's how!

Before beginning, please read about knitting with cotton in the introduction to this chapter (page 103).
BACK
Edging
With cable cast-on (page 96) and smaller needle, cast on 96 (104, 112, 120, 128, 136, 144) sts.
K 2 rows.

EXPERIENCE
- *very easy*
- *simple shaping*
- *simple finishing*

OVERSIZED FIT

Child's 6–8 (10–12, Woman's S, M, L, XL, XXL)

A 39 (42, 45, 49, 52, 56, 58)"
B 22 (25, 28, 28, 28, 28, 28)"
C 23 (26, 29, 29, 29, 29, 29)"

10cm/4"

18   GET CLOSE
22

- *over stitches and garter ridges of Opaque fabric*

You'll need

1 2 **3** 4 5 6

- *light weight*
- *930 (1100, 1300, 1400, 1500, 1600, 1700) yds*
- *cotton or cotton blend*

I used

- *3.75mm/US 5*
- *7mm/US 10½*

Next (decrease) row (WS) Onto larger needle, *k2, slip 1, knit 1, pass slip stitch over (SKP, page 79), repeat from*—72 (78, 84, 90, 96, 102, 108) sts remain.

Sheer 'skirt'

Over sheer areas, end balls of yarn (and begin new ones) at ends of rows (page 38); sew tails into seams.

Beginning with RS row, work Sheer fabric to 7 (8, 9, 9, 9, 9, 9)" from beginning, measured after pressing (while still on needle), and ending with WS row.

You really do need to stop and press the sheer area, according to directions on page 20, before measuring.

Next (increase) row Onto smaller needle, *k1, knit in front and back of next stitch (kf&b, page 57), repeat from*—108 (117, 126, 135, 144, 153, 162) sts on needle.

Opaque body

Work Opaque fabric to 14 (16, 18, 18, 17, 16, 16)" from beginning, ending with WS row. SHORTEN OR LENGTHEN HERE.

Shape armhole

Bind off 22 (22, 19, 24, 28, 32, 37) sts at beginning of next 2 rows—64 (73, 88, 87, 88, 89, 88) sts remain. Continue Opaque fabric to 7½ (8½, 9½, 9½, 10½, 11½, 11½)" above armhole bind-off, ending with WS row.

Shape right back neck

Short row 1 (RS) K15 (19, 24, 23, 24, 24, 24), put next 34 (35, 40, 41, 40, 41, 40) sts onto holder (for center back neck). Turn work (ready to work WS row), leaving 15 (19, 24, 23, 24, 24, 24) sts behind (on needle) for left shoulder (page 114).

Row 2 (and all WS rows) K.

Short row 3 K to 1 st from end, then turn.

Short row 5 K to 2 sts from end, then turn.

Row 7 Bind off 13 (17, 22, 21, 22, 22, 22) sts. Put 2 live sts onto holder with center back neck sts.

Shape left back neck

Return to 15 (19, 24, 23, 24, 24, 24) sts left behind for left shoulder, ready to work RS row.

Row 1 (and all RS rows) K.

Short row 2 K to 1 st from end, then turn.

Short row 4 K to 2 sts from end, then turn.

Row 6 Bind off 13 (17, 22, 21, 22, 22, 22) sts. Put 2 live sts onto holder with center back neck sts.

FRONT

Work as Back to 6 (7, 8, 8, 9, 10, 10)" above armhole bind-off, ending with WS row.

Shape left front neck

Short row 1 (RS) K22 (26, 31, 30, 31, 31, 31), put next 20 (21, 26, 27, 26, 27, 26) sts onto holder (for center front neck). Turn work (ready to work WS row), leav-

Child's 6–8: 5 balls SIRDAR Denim Tweed DK in color #553

Woman's M: 13 skeins TAHKI Cotton Classic in color #3356

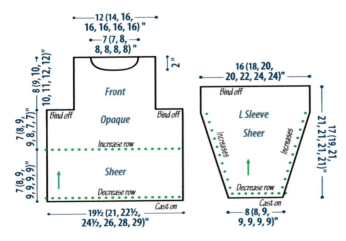

12 (14, 16, 16, 16, 16, 16)"
7 (7, 8, 8, 8, 8, 8)"
2"
8 (9, 10, 10, 11, 12, 12)"
Front
7 (8, 9, 9, 8, 7, 7)"
Bind off   Opaque   Bind off
Increase row
7 (8, 9, 9, 9, 9, 9)"
Sheer
Decrease row
19½ (21, 22½, 24½, 26, 28, 29)"

16 (18, 20, 20, 22, 24, 24)"
Bind off
L Sleeve
Sheer
Increases   Increases
17 (19, 21, 21, 21, 21, 21)"
Decrease row
Cast on
8 (8, 9, 9, 9, 9, 9)"

SALLY'S FAVORITE SUMMER SWEATER

ing 22 (26, 31, 30, 31, 31, 31) sts behind (on needle) for left shoulder.

Row 2 (and all WS rows) K.

Short row 3 K to 2 sts from end, then turn.

Short row 5 K to 4 sts from end, then turn.

Short row 7 K to 5 sts from end, then turn.

Short rows 9, 11, 13, 15 K to 6, then 7, then 8, then 9 sts from end before turning.

Rows 17–19 K13 (17, 22, 21, 22, 22, 22).

Row 20 (WS) Bind off 13 (17, 22, 21, 22, 22, 22) sts.

Put 9 live sts onto holder with center front neck sts.

Shape right front neck

Return to 22 (26, 31, 30, 31, 31, 31) sts left behind for left shoulder, ready to work RS row.

Row 1 (and all RS rows) K.

Rows 2, 4, 6, 8, 10, 12, 14 Repeat directions for Rows 3–15 of left Front neck, working reverse shaping.

> *This means that you will work Row 2 as Row 3 (above), then Row 4 as Row 5 (above), etc.*

Rows 16–20 K13 (17, 22, 21, 22, 22, 22) sts.

Row 21 Bind off 13 (17, 22, 21, 22, 22, 22) sts.

Put 9 live sts onto holder with center front neck sts.

SLEEVES

With cable cast-on and smaller needle, cast on 40 (40, 44, 44, 44, 44, 44) sts.

K 2 rows.

Next (decrease) row Onto larger needle, *k2, SKP, repeat from*—30 (30, 33, 33, 33, 33, 33) sts remain. Beginning with RS row, work Sheer fabric to 2 (2, 3, 3, 3, 3, 3)" from beginning, after pressing (while still on needle), ending with WS row.

Next (increase) row (RS) K2, make 1 (M1, page 79), k to 2 sts remaining, M1, k2.

Continue Sheer fabric for 3 more rows.

Repeat these last 4 rows, working increases at each end of sleeve each 4th row, to 58 (64, 71, 71, 77, 85, 85) sts.

Continue Sheer fabric to 17 (19, 21, 21, 21, 21, 21)" from beginning, after pressing (while still on needle), ending with RS row. SHORTEN OR LENGTHEN HERE.

Next row With larger needles, bind off.

FINISHING

Sew left shoulder seam (stitches to stitches, page 74).

Neck edging

Use smaller needle.

Beginning at right back neck and with RS facing, pick up and k, then immediately bind off, 1 st for each live st plus 1 st for each 2-row step (or ridge) around entire neck edge (page 114).

Sew right shoulder seam.

Sleeve to armhole

> *For perfect results, you need to do a little math! I promise you that it's worth the effort.*

Do the math!

sts in upper Sleeve is 58 (64, 71, 71, 77, 85, 85).

sts in half upper Sleeve is 29 (32, 35, 35, 38, 42, 42).

Find the number of sts that corresponds to your size, and record it as _____sts.

Count the number of ridges along left Front armhole edge—from shoulder seam to bind-off at underarm, and record it as ____ridges.

With a calculator, divide the number of sts (the smaller of the two) by the number of ridges (the larger of the two).

You will get a fraction, something less than 1. (If your result is greater than 1, you have made a mistake and need to redo the last step.)

Go to the Table of Comparative Ratios (page 153), and find the fraction closest to your result. The table gives the practical information you need, telling you how to sew the sts of your upper Sleeve to the ridges of your armhole.

Do the sewing!

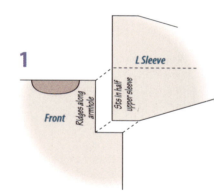

1 Match center upper edge of left Sleeve to left shoulder seam. Sew down left Front armhole, sewing sts of upper Sleeve to ridges of armhole edge (page 42) in the proportion you found by 'doing the math.' As you approach the corner, adjust so upper Sleeve ends at underarm.

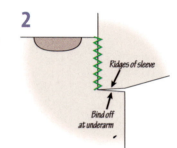

2 At underarm, turn corner. Sew 2 bound-off sts of Front underarm to each ridge of left Sleeve. Return to shoulder, and sew left Sleeve to Back armhole edge and underarm in same manner.

Sew right Sleeve to right Front armhole edge and underarm in same manner.

Sew side and Sleeve seams (ridges to ridges, page 42).

Medium: 10 skeins CLASSIC ELITE Imagine in color # 9213

WHERE'S THE OPAQUE? SWEATER

One successful idea usually generates others—not always as successful (but that's another story). In this case, two design ideas followed the original, oversized pullover (Sally's Favorite Summer Sweater).

What happened first was my thinking about what parts of the body we need to cover and what we do not. This garment, with its sheer back, is the 'minimal' version. But most of us can't afford to be too daring, so there is an unusual bit of shaping at the armholes: the opaque front wraps around slightly, giving more coverage at the sides.

Here is how the Sheer and Opaque fabrics are produced. It's easy to remember, and putting it up front makes the pattern easier to read.

SHEER FABRIC
Right-side (RS) rows Knit (k) all stitches (sts) onto smaller needle.
Wrong-side (WS) rows K all sts onto larger needle.
OPAQUE FABRIC
All rows K all sts with smaller needle(s).

Here's how!
FRONT
Edging
With cable cast-on (page 96) and smaller needles, cast on 101 (110, 122, 134) sts.
K 2 rows.
Next (increase) row Increase 10 sts evenly across row (page 99)—111 (120, 132, 144) sts on needle.
Opaque body
Work Opaque fabric to 9½" from beginning. Determine which is right side (RS) row of cast-on, then end with next wrong side (WS) row. SHORTEN OR LENGTHEN HERE.
Shape armhole
Bind off 10 sts at beginning of next 2 rows—91 (100, 112, 124) sts remain.

WHERE'S THE OPAQUE? SWEATER

STANDARD FIT

S (M, L, XL)

A 36 (40, 44, 47½)"
B 18½ (19, 19½, 20)"
C 30"

10cm/4"

18 **GET GAUGE!**

22

• over stitches
and ridges of
Opaque fabric

You'll need

1 2 **3** 4 5 6

• light weight
• 820 (930, 1040,
1150) yds
  • cotton or
  cotton blend

I used

• 3.75mm/US 5
• 6.5mm/US 10½

Next (decrease) row K1, slip 1, knit 1, pass slip stitch over (SKP, page 79), work to 3 sts remaining, knit 2 together (k2tog, page 57), k1.
K 1 (WS) row.
Repeat these last 2 rows, working decreases at each end of RS rows to 75 (78, 84, 90) sts remaining.
Continue Opaque fabric to 3 (3½, 4, 4½)" above armhole bind-off, ending with RS row.

Sheer yoke

Next (decrease) row Onto larger needle, *k1 SKP, repeat from*—50 (52, 56, 60) sts remain.

> *Over sheer areas, end balls of yarn (and begin new ones) at ends of rows (page 38); sew tails into seams.*

Work Sheer fabric to 3½", measured after pressing (while still on needle), ending with WS row.

> *You really do need to stop and press the sheer area, according to directions on page 20, before measuring.*

Shape left front neck

Short row 1 (RS) K16 (17, 19, 21). Put next 18 sts onto holder (for center front neck). Turn work (ready to work WS row), leaving 16 (17, 19, 21) sts behind for right neck and shoulder (on page 114).

Row 2 (and all WS rows) K.

Short row 3 K to 3 sts from end, then turn.

Short row 5 K to 4 sts from end, then turn.

Short rows 7, 9 K to 5, then 6 sts from end, before turning.

Row 10 K 10 (11, 13, 15).

> *When binding off with smaller needles over Sheer fabric, bind off very loosely.*

Row 11 (RS) Bind off 3 (3, 4, 5) sts at beginning of row, k to end.

Rows 12, 14 K.

Row 13 Bind off 3 (4, 4, 5) sts at beginning of row, k to end.

Row 15 Bind off 4 (4, 5, 5) remaining sts.
Put 6 live sts onto holder with center front neck sts.

Shape right front neck

Return to 16 (17, 19, 21) sts left behind for right neck and shoulder, ready to work RS row.

Row 1 (and all RS rows) K.

Short rows 2, 4, 6, 8 Repeat directions for rows 3–9 of left front neck, working reverse shaping.

> *This means that you will work Row 2 as Row 3 (above), then Row 4 as Row 5 (above), etc.*

Row 9 K 10 (11, 13, 15).

Shape right shoulder

Row 10 (WS) Bind off 3 (3, 4, 5) sts at beginning of row, k to end.

Rows 11, 13 K.

Row 12 Bind off 3 (4, 4, 5) sts at beginning of row, k to end.

Row 14 Bind off 4 (4, 5, 5) remaining sts.
Put 6 live sts onto holder with center front neck sts.

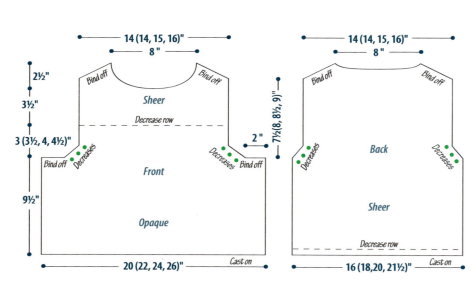

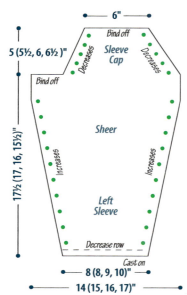

WHERE'S THE OPAQUE? SWEATER

BACK

Edging

With cable cast-on and smaller needles, cast on 80 (92, 100, 108) sts.

K 2 rows.

Next row (RS) Onto larger needle, *k2, SKP, repeat from*—60 (69, 75, 81) sts remain.

Sheer back

Work Sheer fabric to 9½" from beginning, measured after pressing (while still on needle), ending with WS row. SHORTEN OR LENGTHEN HERE.

Shape armhole

Next (decrease) row K1, SKP, work to 3 sts remaining, k2tog, k1.

K 1 (WS) row.

Repeat these last 2 rows, decreasing 1 st at each end of RS rows until 50 (51, 55, 59) sts remain.

Continue Sheer fabric to 7½ (8, 8½, 9)" above beginning of armhole shaping, measured after pressing, ending with RS row.

Shape right back neck

Short row 1 (RS) K12 (13, 15, 17), put next 26 (25, 25, 25) sts onto holder (for center back neck). Turn work (ready to work WS row), leaving 12 (13, 15, 17) sts behind for left shoulder.

Rows 2 & 4 K.

Short row 3 K to 1 st from end, then turn.

Short row 5 K to 2 sts from end, then turn.

Row 6 K 10 (11, 13, 15) sts.

Shape right shoulder

Row 7 (RS) Bind off 3 (3, 4, 5) sts at beginning of row, k to end.

Rows 8 & 10 K.

Row 9 Bind off 3 (4, 4, 5) sts at beginning of row, k to end.

Row 11 Bind off 4 (4, 5, 5) remaining sts.

Put 2 live sts onto holder with center back neck sts.

Shape left back neck

Return to 12 (13,15, 17) sts left behind for left shoulder, ready to work RS row.

Rows 1 & 3 K.

Short row 2 K to 1 st from end, then turn.

Short row 4 K to 2 sts from end, then turn.

Row 5 K.

Shape left shoulder

When binding off with smaller needles over Sheer fabric, bind off very loosely.

Row 6 (WS) Bind off 3 (3, 4, 5) sts at beginning of row, k to end.

Row 7 K.

Row 8 Bind off 3 (4, 4, 5) sts at beginning of row, k to end.

Row 9 K.

Row 10 Bind off 4 (4, 5, 5) remaining sts.

Put 2 live sts onto holder with center back neck sts.

LEFT SLEEVE

Edging

With cable cast-on and smaller needles, cast on 36 (40, 44, 48) sts.

K 2 rows.

Next row (RS) Onto larger needle, *k2, SKP, repeat from*—27 (30, 33, 36) sts remain.

Work Sheer fabric to 8 rows, ending with WS row.

Next (increase) row K2, make 1 (M1, page 79), k to 2 sts remaining, M1, k2.

Continue Sheer fabric for 5 (5, 5, 3) more rows.

Repeat these last 6 (6, 6, 4) rows, increasing at each end of sleeve each 6 (6, 6, 4) th row to 53 (56, 59, 64) sts.

Continue Sheer fabric to 17½ (17, 16, 15)" from beginning, measured after pressing (while still on needle), ending with RS row. SHORTEN OR LENGTHEN HERE.

Shape sleeve cap

Continue Sheer fabric through shaping.

Bind off 7 sts at beginning of next WS row—44 (47, 52, 55) sts remain.

Rows 1, 3, 5 (RS) K2, SKP, work to 4 sts remaining, k2tog, k2.

Rows 2, 4, 6, 7, 8 K.

Repeat these last 8 rows, working decreases 3 out of 4 RS rows until 22 (23, 22, 23) sts remain.

Bind off 2 sts at beginning of next 2 rows.

Bind off remaining 18 (19, 18, 19) sts.

RIGHT SLEEVE

Work as for Left Sleeve to shaping of sleeve cap, ending with WS row.

Shape sleeve cap

Continue Sheer fabric through shaping.

Bind off 7 sts at beginning of next RS row—44 (47, 52, 55) sts remain.
Work 1 (WS) row.
Work as Right Sleeve from Row 1 of Sleeve Cap to end.

FINISHING
Sew left shoulder seam (stitches to stitches, page 74).

Neck edging
Use smaller needle.
Beginning at right back neck, pick up and k, then immediately bind off, 1 st for each live st plus 1 st for each 2-row step (or ridge) around entire neck edge (page 114).
Sew right shoulder seam.

1 **Seam sleeve into armhole**
Sew 7 bound-off sts of Left Sleeve underarm to 10 bound-off sts of right front underarm.

2 Pin center of sleeve cap to shoulder seam. Mark place on armhole to which flat, bound-off edge of sleeve cap extends, and pin edge of sleeve cap to this point.

3 Sew ridges of sleeve cap to ridges of armhole (page 42), easing to fit from underarm to first pin.
Then sew bound-off sts of sleeve cap to remaining ridges of armhole (page 42), ending at second pin.

4 Sew back of Left Sleeve cap to Back armhole in same manner.
Sew Right Sleeve to right armhole in same manner.
Sew side and sleeve seams.

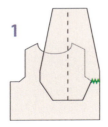
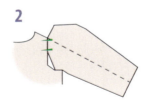
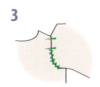
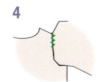

Small: 8 balls REYNOLDS Cantata in color #135

CADDY'S SWEATER

The next 'generation' of this garment moved backwards one step, to something less dressy and with a little more coverage. (The back is like the front—opaque to the yoke.) It's something everyone can wear. My 24-year-old daughter loves it, as does my 59-year-old best friend!

Here is how the Sheer and Opaque fabrics are produced. It's easy to remember, and putting it up front makes the pattern easier to read.

SHEER FABRIC
Right-side (RS) rows Knit (k) all stitches (sts) onto smaller needle.
Wrong-side (WS) rows K all sts onto larger needle.
OPAQUE FABRIC
All rows K all sts with smaller needle(s).

Here's how!
FRONT
Work as for Where's the Opaque? sweater, page 107.

BACK
Edging
With cable cast-on and smaller needles, cast on 81 (88, 102, 112) sts.
K 2 rows.
Next (increase) row Increase 8 sts evenly (page 99) across row—89 (96, 110, 120) sts on needle.
Opaque body
Work Opaque fabric to 9½" from beginning, ending with WS row. SHORTEN OR LENGTHEN HERE.
Shape armhole
Next (decrease) row K1, slip 1, k1, pass slip stitch over (SKP), work to 3 sts remaining, k2tog, k1.
Work 1 (WS) row.
Repeat these last 2 rows, working decreases at each end of RS rows to 75 (78, 84, 90) sts remaining.
Continue Opaque fabric to 3 (3½, 4, 4½)" above beginning of armhole shaping, ending with RS row.
Sheer yoke
Next (decrease) row Onto larger needle, *k1, SKP, repeat from* to 1 st remaining, k1—50 (52, 56, 60) sts remain.

EXPERIENCE

• *easy intermediate*
• *mid-level shaping*
• *mid-level finishing*

STANDARD FIT

S (M, L, XL)

A 36 (40, 44, 48)"
B 18½ (19, 19½, 20)"
C 29"

10cm/4"

18

22

• *over stitches and garter ridges of Opaque fabric*

You'll need

1 2 **3** 4 5 6

• *light weight*
• *920 (1020, 1150, 1280) yds*
• *cotton or cotton blend*

I used

• *3.75mm/US 5*
• *6.5mm/US 10½*

Continue Sheer fabric to 7½ (8, 8½, 9)" above beginning of armhole shaping, measured after pressing, ending with WS row.

Shape right back neck
Short row 1 (RS) K12 (13, 15, 17), put next 26 sts onto holder (for center back neck). Turn work (ready to work WS row), leaving 12 (13, 15, 17) sts behind for left shoulder.
Rows 2 & 4 K.
Short row 3 K to 1 st from end, then turn.
Short row 5 K to 2 sts from end, then turn.
Row 6 K 10 (11, 13, 15) sts.

Shape right shoulder
> *When binding off with smaller needles over Sheer fabric, bind off very loosely.*

Row 7 (RS) Bind off 3 (3, 4, 5) sts at beginning of row, k to end.
Rows 8 & 10 K.
Row 9 Bind off 3 (4, 4, 5) sts at beginning of row, k to end.
Row 11 Bind off 4 (4, 5, 5) remaining sts.
Put 2 live sts onto holder with center back neck sts.

Shape left back neck
Return to 12 (13, 15, 17) sts left behind for left shoulder, ready to work RS row.
Rows 1 & 3 K.
Short row 2 K to 1 st from end, then turn.
Short row 4 K to 2 sts from end, then turn.
Row 5 K 10 (11, 13, 15) sts.

Shape left shoulder
Row 6 Bind off 3 (3, 4, 5) sts at beginning of row, k to end.
Rows 7 & 9 K.
Row 8 Bind off 3 (4, 4, 5) sts at beginning of row, k to end.
Row 10 Bind off 4 (4, 5, 5) remaining sts.
Put 2 live sts onto holder with center back neck sts.

SLEEVES
Work as for Where's the Opaque? sweater.

FINISHING
Sew left shoulder seam (stitches to stitches, page 74).
Neck edging
Use smaller needle.
Beginning at right back neck, pick up and k, then immediately bind off, 1 st for each live st plus 1 st for

each 2-row step (or ridge) around entire neck edge (page 114).
Sew right shoulder seam.

Sleeve into armhole
See drawings on page 111 to help visualize what follows.

1 Sew bound-off sts of Left Sleeve underarm to bound-off sts of right front underarm.

2 Pin center of sleeve cap to shoulder seam. Mark place on armhole to which flat, bound-off edge of sleeve cap extends, and pin edge of sleeve cap to this point.

3 Sew ridges of sleeve cap to ridges of armhole (page 42) from underarm to first pin .

4 Then sew bound-off sts of sleeve cap to remaining ridges of armhole (page 42), ending at second pin.
Sew back of Left Sleeve cap to Back armhole in same manner.
Sew Right Sleeve to right armhole in same manner.
Sew side and sleeve seams.

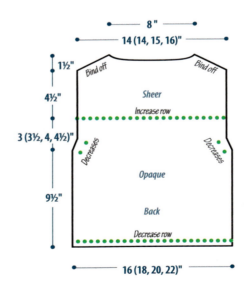

Short rows and Live stitches

WORKING A SHORT ROW

In the garments of this chapter, you will shape a curve then go back and pick up and knit an edging onto it. There are lots of ways to do this, but the simplest is what is done here.

You can shape a neck by working *short rows*. To do this, you turn mid-row, leaving *live stitches* (stitches not bound off) behind. A progression of stitches left behind will shape your curve.

1 To leave three live stitches, knit to three stitches from the end.

PICKING UP AND KNITTING OFF A SHORT ROW

Knitting from the live stitches is easy enough: they're just regular stitches. But if you knit only them, you won't have enough stitches to go around the curve. You need extras.

In the garment patterns that follow, you will be told to knit each of the live stitches and to pick up and knit one stitch between live stitches.

Between the live stitches are stairsteps. They come from the two rows of knitting worked between the stitches left behind. Here, there are two of these steps: the first step is between the three live stitches and the one live stitch; the second step is between the single live stitches.

To pick up and knit the edging, work as follows and with right side facing.
1 Put all the live stitches onto left-hand needle, ready to work a right-side row.

2 Knit the first group of stitches as usual until you are at a two-row step.

3 Put right-hand needle into stitch below next stitch on left-hand needle.

Seaming shaped garments

In this chapter and the one that follows, there are shaped garments that need to be seamed. You have been shown the mechanics of seaming on pages 42 and 74. But with shaped garments, there are sometimes proportions that need to be sorted out, easements that need to occur, puzzles that need assembling. So, in the directions for each of these patterns, detailed instructions are given for the assembling of these shaped pieces.

2 Turn, leaving three live stitches behind.

Three live stitches left behind at the beginning of the row (by the right thumb), shown after knitting the next row

The result of a typical short row, with the stitches taken off the needle: three stitches left once (shown in Steps 1–2), one stitch left once, then one stitch left again, then six rows worked straight, with all remaining stitches bound off.

4 With working yarn, draw through a stitch.

5 Now knit the next stitch on left-hand needle as usual. Repeat Steps 3–5 for the next stairstep.

The result: instead of the five 'live' stitches, there are now seven—one extra for each of the stairsteps.

This two-row step between live stitches is not as tall in garter stitch as it will be in other stitch patterns.

Oops! Despite my best efforts to pick up and knit the right number of stitches around a neck edge, the finished edge looks sloppy. What do I do now? See page 149.

SEAMING A SHAPED SHOULDER SEAM

One kind of shaping that does not require additional assembling instructions is the shaped shoulder. (This shaping occurred in the final two patterns of this chapter, and is shown as a sloped shoulder line on the drawings.) To seam these, just sew stitches to stitches, page 74. When the next stitch to be seamed is two rows below, just go there. Pull your seaming thread taut, every few stitches, to turn the seam allowance to the wrong side.

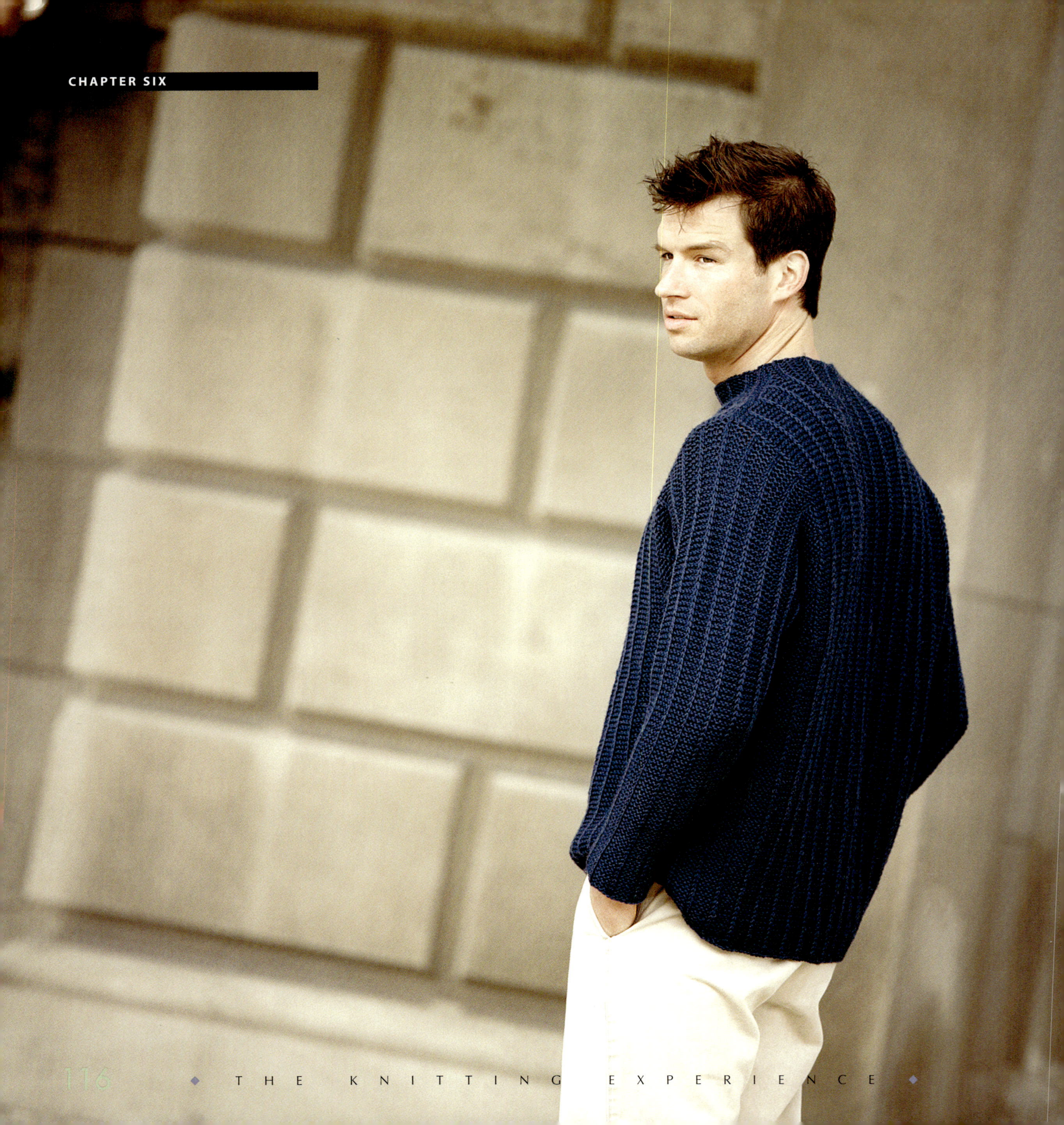

It has been said that there are only two stitches in knitting—the knit stitch and the purl stitch—and that all the wonderful fabrics of knitting are only variations of these.

There is truth to this statement, and a world of fabric possibilities awaits once you learn to purl. The next book in this series will explore some of those fabrics whose classic textures use both knit and purl.

Until then, this chapter offers a textured fabric that doesn't require learning to purl: something for women, something for men, something for children; some in wool, some in cotton, some in a blend; some cardigans, some pullovers, and a top that doesn't know what it is! All are in a neat texture that's accomplished without learning to purl.

CHAPTER SIX

The Patterns

Additional Skills

CHILD'S 6–8: 5 balls REYNOLDS Cabana in color #940

Man's L: 11 balls REYNOLDS Cabana in color #818

CLASSIC MALE CARDIGAN

This stitch pattern has a very classic look, perfect for a father/son duo. The two garments are shown in a bulky-weight cotton blend. This weight works up really quickly, and the cotton content gives it great body and multi-seasonality.

This fabric has slip stitches, at every fifth stitch, on all wrong-side rows. Failure to remember to work them, or to work them in the same place each time, will ruin this fabric.

To learn the stitch pattern, to imbed it in your memory, I suggest you practice it in your gauge swatch.

Here are special directions for your gauge swatch.
- *Cast on 15 sts. (Any cast-on is fine, but you could practice the crochet cast-on, page 74.)*
- *Work Stitch pattern to 15 garter ridges.*
- *Bind off.*
- *Piece should measure 4" x 4", not including cast-on or bind-off.*

Stitch pattern
Right-side (RS) rows Knit (k) all stitches (sts).
Wrong-side (WS) rows K2, *with yarn in front (yf, page 76), slip 1 stitch purl-wise (sl 1 p-wise, page 78), take yarn back (yb), k4, repeat from* to 3 sts remaining, yf, sl 1 p-wise, yb, k2.

Here's how!

BACK
With crochet cast-on, cast on 60 (70, 80, 90, 100, 110) sts onto smaller needle.
Work Stitch pattern to 3 garter ridges.
Change to larger needles, and work Stitch pattern to 14½ (17½, 23, 23½, 23½, 24)" from beginning.
SHORTEN OR LENGTHEN HERE.
Bind off next RS row.

LEFT FRONT
With crochet cast-on, cast on 30 (35, 40, 45, 50, 55) sts onto smaller needle.
Work Stitch pattern to 3 garter ridges.
Change to larger needles, and work Stitch pattern to 9½ (12, 17, 17½, 17½, 18)" from beginning, ending with WS row. SHORTEN OR LENGTHEN HERE.

LOOSE FIT

Child's 6–8 (10–12
Man's M, L, XL, XXL)
A *32 (36, 43, 48, 53, 59)"*
B *16½ (20, 26½, 27,*
27, 27½)"
C *21 (24, 33, 33, 33, 33)"*

10cm/4"

15

- *over stitches and garter ridges of Stitch pattern*
- *with larger needles*

You'll need

- *bulky weight*
- *550 (790, 1250, 1360, 1470, 1600) yds*
- *cotton blend*

- *⅞" buttons, Four (five, six, six, six, six)*

I used

- *5mm/US 8*
- *4mm/US 6*

- *4mm/US F*

Shape V-neck
Next (decrease) row (RS) K to 3 sts remaining, knit two together (k2tog, page 57), k1.
Next row (WS) Work Stitch pattern as established.
For ease in picking up sts for band, do not sl first st of WS rows, even when Stitch pattern demands it.
Repeat last 2 rows, decreasing at neck edge each RS row, to 20 (23, 26, 31, 36, 41) sts remaining.
Continue Stitch pattern to 14½ (17½, 23, 23½, 23½, 24)" from beginning, ending with WS row.
Bind off next RS row.

RIGHT FRONT
Work as Left Front to V-neck shaping.
Shape V-neck
Next (decrease) row (RS) K1, slip 1, knit 1, pass slip stitch over (SKP, page 79), k to end.
Next row (WS) Work Stitch pattern as established.
For ease in picking up sts for band, do not sl last st of WS rows, even when Stitch pattern demands it.
Repeat these last 2 rows, decreasing at neck edge each RS row to 20 (23, 26, 31, 36, 41) sts remaining.
Continue Stitch pattern to 14½ (17½, 23, 23½, 23½, 24)" from beginning, ending with WS row.
Bind off next RS row.

LEFT SLEEVE
With crochet cast-on, cast on 30 (30, 35, 35, 40, 40) sts onto smaller needle.
Work Stitch pattern to 3 garter ridges.
Change to larger needles.
Next (increase) row K1, Make 1 (M1, page 79), work to 1 st remaining, M1, k1—32 (32, 37, 37, 42, 42) sts.
Continue Stitch pattern as established for 5 (3, 5, 3, 3, 3) more rows.
Repeat from*, increasing 1 st at each end of Sleeve each 6 (4, 6, 4, 4, 4) rows, to 54 (72, 81, 87, 90, 96) sts.
Continue Stitch pattern as established to 13 (15, 22, 21, 20, 18½)" from beginning, ending with WS row.
SHORTEN OR LENGTHEN HERE.
Form saddle
Maintain Stitch pattern as established through bind-offs.
Bind off 20 (27, 28, 31, 32, 35) sts beginning next 2 rows—14 (18, 25, 25, 26, 26) sts remain.

Continue Stitch pattern as established to 20 (23, 26, 31, 36, 41) ridges from bind-off, ending with WS row—approximately 5 (6, 7, 8, 9½, 11)".
Finish left front neck
Next (RS) row K7 (9, 12, 12, 13, 13), bind off next 7 (9, 13, 13, 13, 13) sts. Break yarn.
Shape left back neck
Return to remaining 7 (9, 12, 12, 13, 13) sts, ready to work WS row.
Maintain Stitch pattern as established through bind-offs that follow.
For ease in picking up sts for band, do not sl last st of WS rows, even when Stitch pattern demands it.
*Bind off 1 st beginning next WS row, work to end.
Work 1 RS row.
Repeat from* once—5 (7, 10, 10, 11, 11) sts remaining.
Continue Stitch pattern over remaining sts to 2½ (3, 3½, 3½, 3½, 3½)" from beginning of back neck.
Bind off next RS row.

RIGHT SLEEVE
Work as Left Sleeve to 20 (23, 26, 31, 36, 41) ridges from bind-off for saddle, ending with RS row—approximately 5 (6, 7, 8, 9½, 11)".
Finish right front neck
Next (WS) row Maintaining Stitch pattern as established, work 7 (9, 12, 12, 13, 13) sts, bind off next 7 (9, 13, 13, 13, 13) sts. Break yarn.
Shape right back neck
Return to remaining 7 (9, 12, 12, 13, 13) sts, ready to work RS row.
Maintain Stitch pattern as established through bind-offs that follow.
For ease in picking up sts for band, do not sl last st of WS rows.
*Bind off 1 st beginning next RS row, work to end.
Work 1 WS row.
Repeat from* once—5 (7, 10, 10, 11, 11) sts remain.
Continue Stitch pattern over remaining sts to 2½ (3, 3½, 3½, 3½, 3½)" from beginning of back neck.
Bind off next RS row.

CLASSIC MALE CARDIGAN

FINISHING

1 Fit right-angled corner at top of Left Front into right-angled corner at front edge of saddle on Left Sleeve.

2 Start at corner, and sew down sleeve bind-off, sewing bound-off sts of Sleeve to ridges (page 42) down side of Left Front.

3 Return to corner, then sew along front edge of saddle, sewing bound-off sts of Left Front to ridges along edge of left front saddle. (Make whatever adjustments you need, so left front saddle ends at the Left Front neck opening.)

4 Fit right-angled corner at top of Back into right-angled corner at back edge of saddle on Left Sleeve.
Start at corner, and sew down sleeve bind-off, sewing bound-off sts of Sleeve to ridges down side of Back.

5 Return to corner, then sew along back edge of saddle, sewing bound-off sts of Back to ridges along edge of left back saddle. (Make whatever adjustments you need, so end of saddle reaches center back.)
Sew Right Sleeve to Right Front and Back in same manner. Sew left and right saddles together at center back neck (stitches to stitches, page 74).
Sew side and Sleeve seams (ridges to ridges, page 42).

BUTTON BAND

With smaller needle and beginning at center back neck, pick up (page 41) 1 st in each garter ridge along entire Right Front edge.

Row 1 With RS facing and beginning at lower edge of Right Front, pick up and k 1 st in each ridge to point of V, then knit into front and back (kf&b, page 57) of st at point of V, then pick up and k 4 sts for each 3 ridges (by picking up and knitting between garter ridges, see page 41, after each 3rd ridge) up diagonal of V-neck shaping, then pick up and k 1 st in each ridge up straight edge above V-neck shaping, then pick up and k 1 st in each bound-off st around corner of back neck, then pick up and k 1 st in each ridge along saddle to center back neck, ending at seam. Turn.

Rows 2, 4, 6 K to 1 st remaining, yf, sl 1 p-wise.

Rows 3, 5 K.

Row 7 (RS) Bind off all sts.

Place markers on button band for 4 (5, 6, 6, 6, 6) buttons, with the first at point of V, the last just above the lower edge, and the rest spaced evenly between.

BUTTONHOLE BAND

With smaller needle and beginning at lower left edge, pick up 1 st in each garter ridge along entire left front edge, to center back neck.

Row 1 With RS facing and beginning at center back neck, pick up and k as directed for Button band: 1 st in each ridge *except* for bound-off sts (1 st in each bound-off st) *and* diagonal of V-neck shaping (pick up and k 1 st between garter ridges after each 3rd ridge) *and* at point of V (work a kf&b into the st).

Row 2 Sl 1 p-wise, yb, k to end.

Row 3 (begin buttonholes) K to position of first button (as marker on Button band indicates), *yarn over (yo, page 77), k2tog, k to position of next button (as marker on Button Band indicates), repeat from * 2 (3, 4, 4, 4, 4) times more, k to position of final buttonhole, yo, k2tog, k to end. 4 (5, 6, 6, 6, 6) buttonholes made.

Row 4 (end buttonholes) Sl 1 p-wise, yb, k all remaining sts, k through front of yo's (so as not to twist them, page 77).

Row 5 K.

Row 6 Sl 1 p-wise, yb, k to end.

Row 7 (RS) Bind off all sts.

Sew bands together at center back.

Sew buttons to Button Band to correspond to buttonholes.

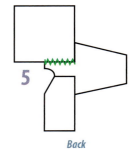

Back

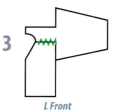

Sleeve back

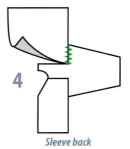

L Front

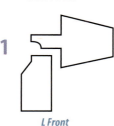

Sleeve front

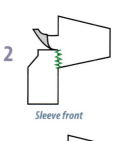

L Front

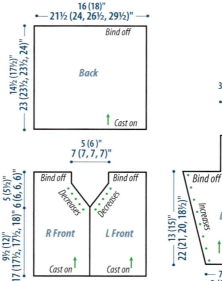

16 (18)"
21½ (24, 26½, 29½)"

Bind off

14½ (17½)"
23 (23½, 23½, 24)"

Back

↑ Cast on

5 (6)"
7 (7, 7, 7)"

Bind off   Bind off

Decreases   Decreases

R Front   **L Front**

Cast on   Cast on

9½ (12)"
17 (17½, 17½, 18)" 6 (6, 6, 6)"
5 (5½)"

3½ (4½)"
6½"

Bind off

Bind-off's

Bind off   Bind off

Increases   **L Sleeve**   Increases

Cast on

13 (15)"
22 (21, 20, 18½)"

7½ (7½)"
9 (9, 10, 10)"

Small: 6 skeins GREAT ADIRONDACK YARN CO. Caribe Irisee in color Leopard

LOTS-OF-CHOICES TOP

I clearly had decisions that I refused to make about this garment. Is it a top or a vest? Is it a V-neck or a round neck? Better yet, let's refuse to make any decisions! All that has to be done is to cut the armholes nice and high (so it could be worn with nothing underneath), to shape both a round neck and a V-neck, and then to put buttons on both front and back (so it could be worn either way).

There is a slip stitch, every fifth stitch, on all wrong-side rows. Failure to remember to work them, or to work them in the same stitch each time, will ruin this fabric.

To learn this stitch pattern, to imbed it in your memory, I suggest you practice it in your gauge swatch.

Here are special directions for your gauge swatch.
 • Cast on 21 stitches (sts). (Any cast-on is fine, but you could practice the crochet cast-on)
 • Work Stitch pattern to 19 garter ridges.
 • Bind off.
 • Piece should measure 4" x 4", not including slip sts at edges, cast-on, or bind-off.

Stitch pattern

Right-side (RS) rows Knit (k) all sts.
Wrong-side (WS) rows *With yarn in front (yf, page 76), slip first st purl-wise (sl 1 p-wise, page 78), take yarn back, (yb), k4, repeat from* to 1 st remaining, yf, sl 1 p-wise.

1 Here's how!

LEFT FRONT/BACK, BELOW ARMHOLE

For clarity, I had to designate one side as the Front and one as the Back, even though you may choose to wear it otherwise. So, for no particular reason, I called the round neck the Front.

With crochet cast-on (page 74), cast on 91 (101, 111, 121, 131) sts.

Work Stitch pattern to 11 (11, 11, 11½, 11½)" from beginning, ending with wrong-side (WS) row.
SHORTEN OR LENGTHEN HERE.

EXPERIENCE

 • *easy intermediate*
 • *mid-level shaping*
 • *minimal finishing*
 • *repetitive stitch pattern*

STANDARD FIT

S (M, L, XL, XXL)

A 35 (39, 44, 48, 52)"
B 18 (18½, 19, 20, 20½)"

10cm/4"

19 — **GET GAUGE!**

19

 • *over stitches and garter ridges of stitch pattern*

You'll need

1 2 3 **4** 5 6

 • *medium weight*
 • *520 (570, 620, 720, 790) yds*
 • *ribbon or tape*

 • *Ten 1" buttons*

I used

 • *4mm/US 7*

 • *4mm/US F*

LOTS-OF-CHOICES TOP

Armhole

Next (RS) row K41 (45, 50, 54, 59) sts. Put these sts just worked onto holder for Left Back. Continuing with RS row, bind off next 9 (11, 11, 13, 13) sts, then k remaining 41 (45, 50, 54, 59) sts.

2 LEFT FRONT, ABOVE ARMHOLE

Next row (WS) Work Stitch pattern as established to 1 st remaining, yf, sl 1 p-wise.

Next (decrease) row (RS) K1, knit two together (k2tog, page 57), k to end.

Repeat these last 2 rows, decreasing 1 st at armhole each RS row, to 31 (36, 36, 41, 41) sts remaining. Continue Stitch pattern without decreases to 4½ (5, 5½, 6, 6½)" above armhole bind-off, ending with RS row.

3 Round neck

Maintain Stitch pattern through bind-offs plus sl the first st of each WS row p-wise, even when this first st is one that you will be binding off.

Bind off 12 sts at beginning next WS row—19 (24, 24, 29, 29) sts remain.

Bind off 2 sts at beginning next 2 WS rows—15 (20, 20, 25, 25) sts remain.

Bind off 1 st at beginning next 4 WS rows—11 (16, 16, 21, 21) sts remain.

Continue Stitch pattern to 6 (6½, 7, 7½, 8)" above armhole bind-off, ending with WS row.

Shoulder

Continuing Stitch pattern, bind off 4 (5, 5, 7, 7) sts at beginning next 2 RS rows, then bind off remaining sts at beginning next RS row.

Place 5 markers for buttons along Left Front edge, with the first ½" below neck edge, the last 1½" above lower edge, and 3 others spaced evenly between.

4 LEFT BACK, ABOVE ARMHOLE

Return to 41 (45, 50, 54, 59) sts on holder. Put sts on needle, ready to work WS row.

Next row (WS) Yf, sl 1 p-wise, continue Stitch pattern as established.

Next (decrease) row (RS) K to 3 sts remaining, slip 1, knit 1, pass slip stitch over (SKP, page 79), k1.

Repeat these last 2 rows, decreasing 1 st at armhole each RS row to 31 (36, 36, 41, 41) sts remaining. Continue Stitch pattern but without decreases to 3 (3½, 4, 4½, 5)" above armhole bind-off, ending with WS row.

5 V-neck

Next decrease row (RS) K1, k2tog, k to end.

Next row (WS) Yf, sl 1 p-wise, yb, work Stitch pattern as established to 1 st remaining, yf, sl 1 p-wise.

Repeat these last 2 rows, decreasing at neck edge until 11 (16, 16, 21, 21) sts remain.

Continue Stitch pattern to 6 (6½, 7, 7½, 8)" above armhole bind-off, ending with RS row.

L Front/Back

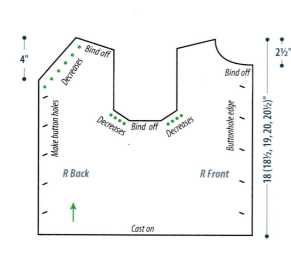

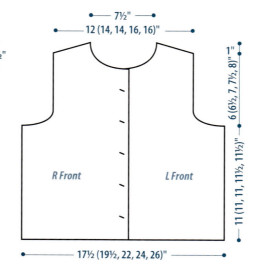

Shoulder

Maintaining Stitch pattern as established through bind-offs, bind off 4 (5, 5, 7, 7) sts at beginning next 2 WS rows, then bind off remaining sts at beginning next WS row. Place 5 markers for buttons along Left Back edge, with the first ½" below V-neck, the last 1½" above lower edge, and 3 others spaced evenly between.

RIGHT FRONT/BACK, BELOW ARMHOLE

This half garment mirrors the left. Neck shapings are on opposite sides to drawings 1–5. The measurement drawing will help you visualize this.

With crochet cast-on, cast on 91 (101, 111, 121, 131) sts. Work Stitch pattern to 1½", ending with WS row.

Begin buttonholes: *Next row (RS)* K3, yarn over (yo, page 77), k2tog (Front edge buttonhole made), k to 5 sts remaining, k2tog, yo (Back edge buttonhole made), k3.

End buttonholes: *Next row* Continuing Stitch pattern, k through back (B, page 56) of yo's (to tighten them, page 77).

Continue Stitch pattern, making Front edge buttonholes (as above) at beginning of RS rows and Back edge buttonholes (as above) at end of RS rows where markers on Left Front/Back indicate, until 11 (11, 11, 11½, 11½)" from beginning, ending with WS row. SHORTEN OR LENGTHEN HERE.

Armhole

Next (RS) row K41 (45, 50, 54, 59) sts. Put these sts just worked onto a holder for Right Front. Continuing with RS row, bind off next 9 (11, 11, 13, 13) sts, then k remaining 41 (45, 50, 54, 59) sts.

RIGHT BACK, ABOVE ARMHOLE

Continue to make Back edge buttonholes (as above) at end of RS rows, where markers on Left Back indicate.

Next row (WS) Continue Stitch pattern as established to 1 st remaining, yf, sl 1 p-wise.

Next (decrease) row (RS) K1, k2tog, k to end.
Repeat these last 2 rows, decreasing 1 st at armhole each RS row to 31 (36, 36, 41, 41) sts remaining. Continue Stitch pattern but without decreases to 3 (3½, 4, 4½, 5)" above armhole bind-off, ending with WS row.

V-neck

Next (decrease) row (RS) K to 3 sts remaining, SKP, k1.
Next row (WS) Yf, sl 1 p-wise, yb, work Stitch pattern as established to end.

Repeat these last 2 rows, decreasing at neck edge until 11 (16, 16, 21, 21) sts remain. Continue Stitch pattern to 6 (6½, 7, 7½, 8)" above armhole bind-off, ending with WS row.

Shoulder

Continuing Stitch pattern, bind off 4, (5, 5, 7, 7) sts beginning next 2 RS rows, then bind off remaining sts beginning next RS row.

RIGHT FRONT, ABOVE ARMHOLE

Return to 41 (45, 50, 54, 59) sts on holder. Put sts on needle, ready to work WS row. Continue to make Front edge buttonholes (as above) at beginning of RS rows, where markers on Left Front indicate.

Next row (WS) Yf, sl 1 p-wise, continue Stitch pattern as established.

Next (decrease) row (RS) K to 3 sts remaining, SKP, k1.

Repeat these last 2 rows, decreasing 1 st at armhole each RS row to 31 (36, 36, 41, 41) sts remaining.
Continue Stitch pattern but without decreases to 4½ (5, 5½, 6, 6½)" above armhole bind-off, ending with WS row.

Round neck

WS rows Yf, sl 1 p-wise, yb, maintain Stitch pattern after bind-offs.
Bind off 12 sts at beginning next RS row—19 (24, 24, 29, 29) sts remain.
Bind off 2 sts at beginning next 2 RS rows—15 (20, 20, 25, 25) sts remain.
Bind off 1 st at beginning next 4 RS rows—11 (16, 16, 21, 21) sts remain.
Continue Stitch pattern as established to 6 (6½, 7, 7½, 8)" above armhole bind-off, ending with RS row.

Shoulder

Maintaining Stitch pattern through bind-offs, bind off 4 (5, 5, 7, 7) sts at beginning next 2 WS rows, then bind off remaining sts at beginning next WS row.

FINISHING

Sew shoulder seams (stitches to stiches, page 42).
Sew buttons to Left Front and Left Back edges to correspond to buttonholes.

Medium: 5 balls GARNSTUDIO Passion in color #7

CHILD'S 8: 9 balls MISSION FALLS 1824 Cotton in color #102

KNIT-DOWN, MADE-TO-MEASURE JUMPERS

In this book you have seen garments knit up from the bottom, knit from side to side, and knit with combinations of these two methods. What option remains? Right! Knitting down from the top!

Knitting down from the top allows you to knit to the perfect length, for whatever body you are fitting. Why we don't always knit that way? Because it's not so easy when there is neck shaping. But for these funnel-necked garments, without neck shaping, it's a neat option.

These patterns are written differently than those you have seen so far. I don't offer a range of sizes: you will decide—at the shoulders and at the underarms—what size to knit. Sometimes you are given one option, sometimes four, sometimes six. Since it's not a fitted garment, all you have to do is choose the measurement closest to what you want, then follow the easy steps. I hope you enjoy the experience, because—as you proceed with your knitting—it's good to understand that you always have choices ... and then to have the confidence to make them!

The chest measurements (A) are unisex, and they cover all choices available. You will choose one of these sizes when you cast on at the underarm in Step 4.
The length measurements (B, C) are for a 5'4"–5'6" woman, for a 6' man, and for a child's size 8. The measurements shown on the drawing are for the model garments: child's 8 (woman's M, man's L). You will make the garment any length you want.

This fabric has slip stitches, at every 5th stitch, on all wrong-side rows. Failure to remember to work them, or to work them in the same place each time, will ruin this fabric.
To learn the Stitch pattern, to imbed it in your memory, I suggest you practice it in your gauge swatch.

EXPERIENCE
- *easy intermediate*
- *repetitive stitch pattern*
- *some math required*
- *simple shaping*
- *simple finishing*

LOOSE FIT

**Child's: 6–10
(S, M, L, XL, XXL)**

A *32 (38, 42, 47, 52, 57)"*
B *16 for child's 8
(20" for woman's,
28" for man's)*
C *23½ for child's 8
(29" for woman's,
33" for man's)*

10cm/4"

16   **GET GAUGE!**
16

- *over stitches and garter ridges of stitch pattern*
- *using larger needles*

You'll need

1 2 3 **4** 5 6

- *medium weight*
- *child's 6 (8, 10):
600 (700, 800) yds*
- *woman's: (900, 1100, 1300, 1500, 1700) yds*
- *man's: (1100, 1300, 1500, 1700, 1900) yds*
- *anything*

I used

- *5mm/US 8*
- *4mm/US 6 (optional)*

Here are special directions for your gauge swatch.
- *Cast on 15 sts. (Any cast-on is fine, but you could practice the crochet cast-on, page 74.)*
- *Work Stitch pattern to 16 garter ridges.*
- *Bind off.*
- *Piece should measure 3¾" wide and 4" tall, not including cast-on and bind-off.*

Stitch pattern

Right-side (RS) rows Knit (k) all stitches (sts).
Wrong-side (WS) rows K2, *with yarn in front (yf, page 76), slip 1 stitch purl-wise (sl 1 p-wise, page 78), take yarn back (yb), k4, repeat from* to 3 sts remaining, yf, sl 1 p-wise, yb, k2.

Here's how!

BACK

1 Neck

For ALL sizes With crochet cast-on, cast on 35 stitches (sts) onto larger needle.
Continuing on larger needles, work Stitch pattern to 1½" for crew neck or 3" for mock turtleneck, ending with WS row.

2 Shoulders

You have four choices here. Measure the actual shoulder width of the wearer, then choose the closest measurement.
With e-wrap cast-on (page 10), cast on sts for shoulders as follows.
For 13" shoulders Cast on 2 sts at beginning next 8 rows—51 sts.
For 15" shoulders Cast on 4 sts at beginning next 2 rows, 3 sts at beginning next 6 rows—61 sts.
For 18" shoulders Cast on 5 sts at beginning next 2 rows, 4 sts at beginning next 4 rows, then 5 sts at beginning next 2 rows—71 sts.
For 20" shoulders Cast on 5 sts at beginning next 2 rows, then 6 sts at beginning next 6 rows—81 sts.

3 Armholes

To maintain Stitch pattern as established, WS rows now will be as follows: *sl 1 p-wise, yb, k4, yf, repeat from*, sl 1 p-wise.

You will not be able to work yf, sl 1 p-wise in your last e-wrap cast-on st (the first st of your first armhole WS row). For the first row only, k this st instead.
Work Stitch pattern with sl-st edges for all following WS rows to desired armhole depth, ending with WS row.
Suggestions for armhole depth for child's 8 (woman's M, man's L) are shown on drawing.

4 Underarms

You have six choices here. Measure the chest of the wearer, divide by two, then choose a width that is at least 2" larger.
With e-wrap cast-on, cast on sts at underarm as follows.
For 16" width (child's 6–10) You need a total of 65 sts, so subtract number of sts now on needle from 65, divide remainder by 2, and this is the number of sts you need to cast on at the beginning of the next 2 rows.
For 19" width (size S) You need a total of 75 sts, so subtract number of sts now on needle from 75, divide remainder by 2, and this is the number of sts you need to cast on at the beginning of the next 2 rows.
For 21" width (size M) You need a total of 85 sts, so subtract number of sts now on needle from 85, divide remainder by 2, and this is the number of sts you need to cast on at the beginning of the next 2 rows.
For 23½" width (size L) You need a total of 95 sts, so subtract number of sts now on needle from 95, divide remainder by 2, and this is the number of sts you need to cast on at the beginning of the next 2 rows.
For 26" width (size XL) You need a total of 105 sts, so subtract number of sts now on needle from 105, divide remainder by 2, and this is the number of sts you need to cast on at the beginning of the next 2 rows.
For 28½" width (size XXL) You need a total of 115 sts, so subtract number of sts now on needle from 115, divide remainder

5

3, 4

2

1

Woman's M: 13 balls MISSION FALLS 1824 Wool in color #13

by 2, and this is the number of sts you need to cast on at the beginning of the next 2 rows.

5 Back, below armhole
To maintain Stitch pattern as established, it should be worked as originally written (with k2 at beginning and end of all WS rows).
Work to 1" short of desired length.
Optional To reduce garment width slightly at lower edge, work on smaller needles for final 1".
Bind off next RS row.

FRONT

Now work a second piece, exactly as the first.

If you count the number of sl sts along the Back armhole, and make the same number of sl sts along the Front armhole, your sleeves will be the same size, and you'll feel like a genius!

Shoulders seams
Designate one piece as the Back.
Do all of the following with RS facing.
Connect right shoulders
On Back, using larger needles and beginning at right armhole edge, pick up and k (page 40) the following: 1 st at shoulder sl-st edge, 1 st for every cast-on st along shoulders, 1 st for every ridge along side of neck, 1 st for cast-on row at neck edge.

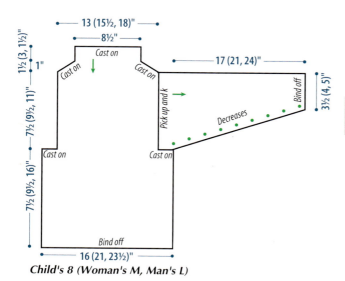

— 13 (15½, 18)" —
— 8½" —
Cast on
13 (15½, 18)"
1½ (3, 3½)"
1"
Cast on
Cast on
Cast on
Cast on
7½ (9½, 11)"
7½ (9½, 16)"
Pick up and k
Decreases
— 17 (21, 24)" —
Bind off
3½ (4, 5)"
Bind off
— 16 (21, 23½)" —

Child's 8 (Woman's M, Man's L)

Next row (WS) K all sts. Break thread. Put sts onto spare needle of any size, with neck st at point end of needle (if using straight needle).
On Front, using larger needles and beginning at right neck edge, pick up and k the following: 1 st for cast-on row at neck edge, 1 st for every ridge along side of neck, 1 st for every cast-on st along shoulders, 1 st at shoulder sl-st edge.
Next row K.

6 Work three-needle bind-off (page 129) Hold Back and Front with WS together. Beginning of row is at neck edges. With larger needle, knit two together (k2tog, page 57), one from each needle, *then k2tog, one from each needle again; now pass first st over second (in usual manner for binding off), repeat from* until all sts have been bound off. Break thread, and draw through remaining st.

Connect left shoulders
Work as above, beginning at neck edge for Back (with these sts put onto spare needle after 2 rows) and beginning at armhole edge for Front. For this three-needle bind-off, beginning of row is at armhole edges.

7 SLEEVES

Work them one at a time, but work them exactly the same. It doesn't matter which you start with.
Beginning at corner where sts were cast on for underarm, with RS facing and with larger needle, pick up and k the following: 1 st at corner, 1 st in back of every sl st (page 78) along armhole edge, 1 st at three-needle bind-off, 1 st in back edge of every sl st along armhole edge, 1 st at corner where sts were cast on for underarm.

Now you need to establish the Stitch pattern for your Sleeve. Have a cup of tea, take a deep breath, and keep smiling through this next bit.
Next row (WS) Find st on needle that aligns with shoulder three-needle bind-off. For the next and all following WS rows, this should be treated as a slip stitch (yf, sl 1 p-wise). Every 5th stitch, from this one to the beginning of this WS row, should also be a slip stitch (yf, sl 1 p-wise).
So, count back by 5—noting that these 5th sts are your sl sts—from the three-needle bind-off. There will be 0–4 sts remaining.

K these 0–4 sts, then work first yf, sl 1 p-wise, yb. Now work rest of row as *k4, yf, sl 1 p-wise, yb, repeat from*.

Knit the 0–4 sts remaining at the end of the row.

Make note of how many sts are on needles for upper sleeve.

Work Stitch pattern as established for 3", ending with WS row.

Next (decrease) row (RS) K1, slip 1, knit 1, pass slip stitch over (SKP, page 79), k to 3 sts remaining, k2tog, k1—2 sts decreased.

Continue Stitch pattern for 5 rows.

Repeat these last 6 rows, decreasing 1 st at each end of sleeve each 6th row, 10 times. (You will have 20 fewer sts than Sleeve began with.)

Next (decrease) row (RS) K1, SKP, k to 3 sts remaining, k2tog, k1.

Continue Stitch pattern for 3 rows.

Repeat these last 4 rows, decreasing 1 st at each end of Sleeve each 4th row, to desired number of stitches at cuff.

The number of sts for the cuff is not really about the wrist: it's about getting the cuff over the hand. If your sts are not already on a circular needle, slip them onto one, and wrap sts around the wearer's hand, to find the minimum number of sts that will allow the hand to pass through.

Suggestions for sts at cuff are 29 for a child, 33 for a slim woman, 37 sts for a slim man, 41–45 sts for larger sizes.

Work straight (without further decreases) to 1" short of desired length.

Work on smaller needles for 1".

Bind off next RS row.

FINISHING

Sew side and sleeve seams (ridges to ridges, page 42), leaving 2" un-seamed between Front and Back at lower edges, if desired.

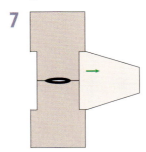

7

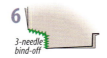

6

3-needle
bind-off

Man's L: 18 balls MISSION FALLS 1824 Wool in color #30

Man's L: 19 balls MISSION FALLS 1824 Cotton in color #102

Maintaining a stitch pattern

A *stitch pattern* usually requires you to do something within a row other than just knitting across. (For example, in this chapter, you produce vertical lines in a garter-stitch fabric by slipping every fifth stitch on wrong-side rows.) *Maintaining a stitch pattern* means not messing it up! (For example, if you put the slip stitch in the fourth rather than the fifth stitch, you'll mess up the vertical produced by the slip stitches.)

To maintain a stitch pattern, it is helpful to place markers on your needle—three or four places across the row—to make sure you're getting the stitch pattern right.

To maintain a stitch pattern through a shaped piece of knitting—an armhole, a V-neck, a sleeve—is more of a challenge. After increases or decreases, the stitch count changes. (In this chapter, the slip stitches are either closer to both edges because you have decreased, or farther away from the edges because you have increased.)

Here's how to maintain a stitch pattern through increases and decreases.
- Do all of this on the row (right-side or wrong-side) on which the pattern is set. (In this chapter, it would be on wrong-side rows.)
- Place a marker before the closest-to-the-edge 'pattern' stitch. (In this chapter, it would be before the first slip stitch.)
- As increases are worked, this pattern stitch will eventually be more than one pattern repeat from the edge.
  As soon as this happens, replace the marker to before the *now* closest-to-the-edge pattern stitch.
- As decreases are worked, this closest-to-the-edge pattern stitch will eventually disappear.
  As soon as this happens, replace the marker to before the *now* closest-to-the-edge pattern stitch.

To maintain the stitch pattern of this chapter is a bit of a challenge. The right-side rows are easy enough: every stitch is knit, so even shaping (increasing or decreasing) is not difficult. The challenge comes on wrong-side rows and where every fifth stitch is slipped. While these slip stitches are visible on the right side, they're not so visible on the wrong side. But it's on the wrong-side rows that you have to remember to work them . . . in the same stitch every time . . . even through shaping.

The three-needle bind-off

In this maneuver, you seam stitches to stitches and bind them off, all in the same motion. It can be used with the bind-off to the wrong side, simply functioning as a seam. Or it can be used with the bind-off to the right side, as a decorative detail.

IF USED DECORATIVELY

1 Leave stitches of one piece on needle, ending with a right-side row.

2 Leave stitches of other piece on needle, ending with a wrong-side row.

3 Hold pieces with wrong sides together.

4 With a third needle, knit two together, one from each needle.

5 Knit two together again, one from each needle.

6 Pass first stitch on right-hand needle over second, binding off one stitch in the usual manner. Repeat Steps 5–6 until all stitches have been bound off.

The finished seam, from the right side

The three-needle bind-off can be used whenever you want to seam stitches to stitches. Lots of knitters use this for their shoulder seams, but unless I am using it to be decorative, I prefer the tightness of sewn seams. However, it is a cool trick, and I am sure you will find uses for it! (In the garments of this chapter, I have used this bind-off decoratively.)

IF NOT USED DECORATIVELY

Work Steps 1–6 except that you will hold pieces with right sides together. Here's what the finished seam looks like from the right side.

SALLY'S TOP 10 LIST OF MOST SIGNIFICANT KNITTING DISCOVERIES

There is much that knitting has taught me. Some of the lessons don't apply beyond the knitting that sits on my needles. But some apply more broadly and have made the universe a friendlier place.

10 Always, always have some easy knitting on needles, ready to take anywhere. (Good idea to carry an extra knitting needle in case you lose one.)

9 If it's not a place I can knit, it's probably not a place I want to be. (Though I spent most of my childhood carsick, I can knit in the car as long as we're on a straight, flat stretch . . . and I'm not driving.)

8 If I don't find time to knit each day, there's something wrong with how I'm living (and I'll get real cranky). (This also applies to getting enough sleep.)

7 Teachers are everywhere. (I will be forever grateful to Della Kinghorn for teaching me the pencil hold, in the kitchen of the Sault Sainte Marie Golf and Country Club in my 17th summer.)

6 Students are more important than teachers. (I never learn anything so well as when I teach it.)

5 The decisions made in the first hour are hugely important to the success of the finished product. (See the Choices chapter that follows.)

4 Mistakes are an opportunity to learn and be creative: a career choice can come of this. (In my case, it was an inability to match the gauge of patterns. I did not know to use smaller needles so, at age 11, I began to design.)

3 Persistence is valuable. (Winston Churchill is reported to have said, "Creativity is the ability to move from one failure to another with no loss of enthusiasm.")

2 Even though persistence is valuable and it's fun to finish, there are times when the piece has nothing more to teach, so it's okay to rip it out or give it away, and move on.

1 The journey is more important than the destination.

Choices

How to make successful garments

The choices we make

Consider the choices you make in the first hour of a project: color, yarn, needles, garment size. These decisions have everything to do with the successful outcome of the hours of knitting that follow. This chapter is about these decisions.

In a simple world, there would be no choices. You would pick a pattern, use the yarn and color shown, know exactly what size to knit, and get exactly those measurements using the needle size the designer recommends.

But the world isn't like that, and neither is knitting. Sometimes the recommended yarn isn't available, you prefer another color, the tension on your yarn is slightly different than the designer's, or your height is not the 5'4" standard.

What to do? Embrace the choices that knitting offers, and proceed with the steps that follow.

Choosing a color

It may seem odd that color choice appears before anything else, but here's why. Color is very powerful. Research has shown that 80% of people who knit a given garment do so in the same color as the model garment. This means that only 20% of knitters can imagine it in a different color. So, if you are part of this vast majority, and you don't like the color in which the designer shows the piece, you won't knit it! This is a testament to the power of color, but you may overlook some wonderful garments.

The pattern you choose to knit will be shown in a particular color. **This is not necessarily the color you ought to buy.**

When a garment in this book is shown in a particular color, it's not because that's the best color for that garment. I may have chosen a color only I like (not your favorite). Or I may have chosen a color because it works with the other pieces in that chapter (with which it is photographed). Or I may have chosen a color because I feared I had neglected it. (Oops, no blue, better knit something in blue.) Can you see how arbitrary this is?

To override the tremendous influence of color, make a black-and-white photocopy of the model garment. If you like it, then knit it—in a color you adore!

Sometimes we pick a color that should look good on us, but when it's knit, the garment does not. What's the deal here?

It may not actually be about the color; it might be about the yarn. Is it shiny or matte? Do you know which looks better on you? One will certainly look better, and the other might look quite awful. Find out what works, and incorporate this into your choice.

Choosing a yarn

For the garments as shown, the brand and the name by which the yarn is known is in the caption.

The pattern you choose to knit will be shown in a particular yarn. **This is not necessarily the yarn you ought to buy.**

YARN SUBSTITUTION

You may not like the yarn I chose. You may be sensitive to it. (Always test the yarn against your skin; if it doesn't feel good, don't use it.) You might prefer to spend less, or the yarn might not be available. (Your yarn shop will be glad to suggest alternatives.)

Yarn substitution is part of knitting. And if you attend to what follows, you'll have fun with it and make the best substitutions possible.

HOW TO KNOW WHAT TYPE OF YARN TO CONSIDER

Every pattern in this book tells you what type of yarn you should use: the vitals column will say *cotton blend,* or *soft wool,* or *novelty yarn.* You will learn easily enough how to find the type of yarn suggested—by asking, by touching, and by checking labels for fiber content.

HOW TO KNOW WHAT WEIGHT OF YARN TO CONSIDER

Every pattern in this book tells you what weight of yarn you should use: the vitals column will give both a number and a word (for example, 4/medium weight). But if you walk into a yarn shop and ask for a 4/medium-weight yarn, many retailers may not know what you mean. What's this about?

These numbers and terms are part of a new standardized system for classifying yarn weights being introduced into the knitting world. They simplify a messy and confusing system, and here's what they mean:

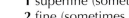

1 2 3 4 **5** 6
• *bulky weight*

1 superfine (sometimes known as sock, fingering, or baby)
2 fine (sometimes known as sport or baby)
3 light (sometimes known as DK/double knitting or light worsted)
4 medium (sometimes known as worsted, afghan, or aran)
5 bulky (sometimes known as chunky, craft, or rug)
6 super bulky (sometimes known as bulky or roving)

For the weight of yarn you need, look at these words by which it is sometimes known. Then look at your pattern for the following additional information: the stitch gauge over 4" and the needle size I used.

You now have three pieces of information with which to work: a name by which the yarn is sometimes known, a stitch gauge that is usual for that yarn, and a needle size that is usual for that yarn. Look at the label of the yarn you are considering. In some form or other, some or all of this information will be there. When you find matching information, you've found a yarn to consider.

I would have a difficult time insisting you always spend lots on yarn. Yes, there are very expensive yarns—and I've used some of them in this book. And there are also very inexpensive yarns—and I've used some of them in this book.

Price does not always correspond with quality. But natural fibers do tend to be more expensive than synthetics, and they do tend to wear better.

Yarns that do not wear well get scruffy-looking. They pill, they stretch and don't come back to shape. Ask the yarn shop owner if the yarn you're considering will wear well. Or buy one ball with which to knit a test piece. Treat it, torture it, see if it holds up through what you would normally subject it to.

Can you see why there is such confusion with respect to yarn weights? Some of the same words appear in more than one weight category! No wonder a standardized system is necessary!

The stitch gauge you see on the label will probably be given over stockinette stitch. Our stitch gauges are usually given over garter stitch. Don't worry about this difference; it doesn't affect the work you'll do for the patterns in this book.

WHAT IF THE RELEVANT INFORMATION ISN'T ON THE LABEL?

Here is a neat test you can use to compare yarns.

Even when you find a yarn whose label gives you the same name or stitch gauge or needle size as your pattern, you don't have to trust this information.

Here's how to ensure perfect results.
1 Find the yarn that was used in the model garment.
2 Employ the substitution test, comparing the yarn used to the yarn you are considering.
3 If the yarn you are considering passes this test, then you've found a yarn the same weight as the one used in the model garment.

1 Find a sample of the correct weight of yarn and a sample of the yarn of unknown weight.

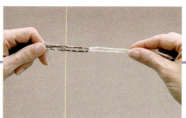

2 Loop the two yarns through each other.

3 Twist the yarns in opposite directions. Hold one end in your teeth (or have someone else hold it), and run your hand over the join. If you feel no change in bulk, the test yarn is the same weight. If you feel a change in bulk, it is not.

So far, you're just considering a yarn based upon its type and weight. There is more you need to consider before buying yarn: which needles, your gauge, which size garment you will knit, and how much yarn you will need.

Choosing needles

WHAT KIND OF NEEDLES?

There are three kinds of needles: straight, circular, and double-pointed (dpn). Here is how they are most commonly used.

Straight needles are only used for flat knitting, in which you work a right-side row, turn your piece, then work a wrong-side row; the garment pieces are worked back and forth and are usually seamed.

Circular needles are not just for circular knitting. I work large, flat pieces on them. The advantage is that you can't lose your needle (and your stitches) as easily as you might on double-pointed or straight needles. The disadvantage is that the cable—the length that joins the points—can be kinked. (To unkink the cable, soak it in the hottest water you can, then pull straight.)

Circular needles can be used for flat knitting (working as you do on straight needles), or they can be used for tubular knitting in which you work continuously around the piece; the garment pieces are worked in rounds and may not require seaming.

Double-pointed needles are most often used for small tubular knitting (working as you do on circular needles) in which you work continuously around small projects like socks, gloves, mitts, and hats. (These needles can come in sets of four or five: we recommend sets of five. See page 60 for a discussion of using dpns.)

How you manage your yarn, hold your needles, and support your knitting will determine which needles you prefer. Until you find out what works for you, practice on whatever you can find: a friend's, the yarn shop's, some treasure from the attic.

WHAT KIND OF NEEDLES FOR WHICH PROJECT?

In most of the patterns that follow, you can use straights or circulars. When it doesn't matter, you will see the straight needle icon. When you need to use circulars or dpns, you will see the icons for these needles.

WHAT NEEDLE MATERIAL?

There are various materials from which knitting needles can be made (metal, wood, plastic, casein, etc.), and there is no way to predict which is best . . . for you, for how you hold your yarn, for the yarn you choose, for your budget, for the project you are knitting. Some will be too slippery, some will be too sharp, some will be too sticky, some will be too blunt . . . and some will be just right. You'll probably borrow or collect a variety until you determine what works for you.

WHAT NEEDLE SIZE?

The pattern you choose to knit will tell you the needle size I used. **This size is not necessarily the size you ought to use.** It is only appropriate if you knit to the same gauge as I do.

Getting gauge

WHAT IS GAUGE, AND WHY DOES IT MATTER?

Gauge is the relationship of stitches and rows to a standard measure recommended by the pattern. If you knit the piece to that gauge, your garment will work up to the measurements of the pattern; if you knit to a different gauge, your garment will not.

In this book's patterns, you are given gauge information in the vitals column. Here's how to interpret that information.

10cm/4"

13

• over stitches and garter ridges
• after blocking

• Gauge is measured over 10cm/4": gauge is almost always measured this way.
• In the bullet you will see the stitch pattern you should be working: here, the gauge is measured over *garter stitches and ridges*.
• The number at the bottom of the grid is the number of stitches you should have over 4": here, it's 13.
• The number at the left of the grid is the number of ridges (or often, rows) you should have over 4": here, it's 13. (Remember that 1 garter ridge = 2 rows of knitting.)
• Additional bullets tell you how to treat your piece before measuring: here, it says *after blocking*.

How do you know that you are getting this right? You make a gauge swatch.

In my classes, I have met knitters who swear they never knit a gauge swatch. And I laughingly respond, "But then you give away garments, don't you—to whomever they fit." They laugh in return, and say, "Yup!"

If these are the rules by which you are willing to abide, fine. But if you are not willing to take these risks, if you want no surprises, then make a gauge swatch.

WHAT IS A GAUGE SWATCH?

A gauge swatch is a trial piece of knitting. To make sure you can match the gauge of the pattern, make a gauge swatch before you begin your garment.

In this book, you will see three different gauge icons. Here's how to interpret them.

 **GET GAUGE!** Make a gauge swatch and match the pattern gauge; otherwise, your piece won't fit in the way you expect.

 **GET CLOSE** Make a gauge swatch and get close to the pattern gauge; the piece is such that exact fit is not terribly important.

 Make a gauge swatch just to make sure you're close to the pattern gauge range; if you fall within this range, you'll get measurements close to what we offer, but this is a piece for which final measurements don't much matter.

HOW DO YOU MAKE A GAUGE SWATCH?

Before you begin your garment, take one ball of yarn to work this trial piece.

What needle size do you use for your gauge swatch? As a starting point, try the needles I used (as shown in the vitals column) or those shown on the yarn label.

Now proceed as follows. (By the way, what follows is for making a gauge swatch in garter stitch—to which this book is dedicated. For other stitch patterns, the rules change. Ask for help.)

1 Cast on the number of stitches given in the gauge information. (If it says 15 stitches, cast on 15 stitches. If it says 14–16 stitches, cast on 16 stitches—the highest number in the range.)

2 Knitting all stitches all rows, work the number of ridges given in the gauge information. (If it says 12 ridges, work 12 ridges/24 rows. If it says 11–13 ridges, work 13 ridges/26 rows—the highest number in the range.) Bind off all stitches.

3 Treat the piece as directed in the pattern before measuring. (If there are no additional instructions, do nothing.)

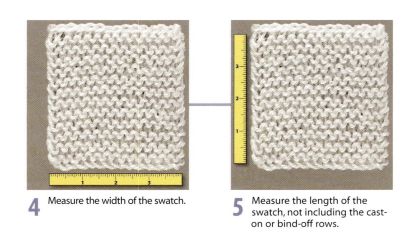

4 Measure the width of the swatch.

5 Measure the length of the swatch, not including the cast-on or bind-off rows.

DID YOU GET GAUGE?
- If you need to GET GAUGE, then your piece should measure 4" x 4".
- If you need to GET CLOSE, then your piece should measure 3¾–4¼" in either direction.
- If you were given a range, your piece should measure 3¾–4¾" in either direction.

If any of the above are the case, your work is done. This is the needle size you use. Proceed to Choosing a garment size, page 138.

Did you get less than the measurement you needed? If so, then your knitting is tight, and you need to work another swatch on larger needles.

Did you get more than the measurement you needed? If so, then your knitting is loose, and you need to work another swatch on smaller needles.

WHAT IS MEANT BY SMALLER OR LARGER NEEDLES?
There are two numbers by which knitting needles are described: the size and the length.

The length is about how long the needle is, and it will have a unit of measure—inches or centimeters (cm) —associated with it: a circular needle may be 24"; a straight needle may be 14"; a double-pointed needle may be 6".

The size is about the thickness of the needle, and it may have a unit of measure associated with it: a needle may be a 4.5mm, or it may be just a 7. The size can be anywhere from 0000 to 15, and it can be a whole number (4) or a fraction (4.5). How do you sort this out?

If you are working with US or metric sizes, then the larger the number, the larger the size. (In these systems, an 8 or an 11mm are large needles.) To the right is a conversion chart for metric and US sizes.

If there is no number on your needle, you may use a needle gauge (usually a small ruler with graduated holes) to determine its size.

Did you not get the measurement you needed? Do not despair! There is nothing wrong with your knitting! It's okay to knit differently than the designer. Also, the yarn can make a difference. You could knit to the suggested gauge just fine with wool but have a difficult time with more slippery yarns.

I am a Canadian, and we 'went metric' a long while back. I'm quite used to this system now. But I teach in the US a lot, so I am always having to convert back and forth. And then there are all those needles of my English grandmother . . . which don't make sense to many now that the English have also 'gone metric.' Oh well, another opportunity to celebrate diversity.

Needle sizes

Metric	US
10	15
9	13
8	11
7.5	
7	
6.5	10½
6	10
5.5	9
5	8
4.5	7
4	6
3.75	5
3.5	4
3.25	3
3	
2.75	2
2.25	1
2	0

IF YOUR GAUGE WAS OFF, HOW MUCH SMALLER OR LARGER DO THE NEEDLES NEED TO BE?
When you need to use smaller or larger needles, you'll have to decide how *much* smaller or larger, and this is mostly a matter of experience. If your gauge is wildly off, then try two or even three sizes up or down. If your gauge is only slightly off, then go to the very next size.

But be careful here. One size smaller than an American 8 is indeed a 7, but one size larger than an American 10 is a 10½! One size smaller than a metric 9 is an 8, but one size larger than a metric 4 is a 4.5. The conversion chart is a necessary piece of equipment, and it offers both the relationship between the different systems and a list of all sizes readily available.

WHEN IS YOUR GAUGE SWATCH DONE?
When you produce a piece that measures 4" x 4", or close enough for your purposes (as discussed on the previous page), your gauge swatch is done, and you know the needle size you should use.

If, after a couple of tries, you get the recommended number of stitches but a slightly different number of rows, use the needle size that gives you the recommended number of stitches, and don't worry about the rows. Most knitting patterns determine length by a number of inches, not by a number of rows. Get as close as you can to the row gauge suggested, remembering that the stitch gauge is more important.

Choosing a garment size

You won't know how much yarn to buy until you determine which garment size you ought to make.

The garments that follow are offered in different sizes and with their familiar designations: S, M, L, XL, XXL. These size designations refer to girth. For now, ignore all measurements for length.

STANDARD SIZES
How do the sizes S-XXL relate to actual body size? The sizes are based on standard bust/chest measurements, as shown here.

This information helps you know what size you really are. But we don't usually wear garments that are our actual bust/chest measurement, do we? What is the relationship between the body measurement and the finished garment measurement?

Standard bust/chest measurements

Size	Women	Men
S	32–34"	34–36"
M	36–38"	38–40"
L	40–42"	42–44"
XL	44–46"	46–48"
XXL	48–50"	50–52"

	Children
0–3 mos	16"
6 mos	17"
12 mos	18"
2–4	21–23"
6–8	25–27"
10–12	28–30"

STANDARDS OF FIT

There are three 'fit' possibilities that appear in this book. Here is an explanation of their icons, as they appear in the vitals column of each pattern.

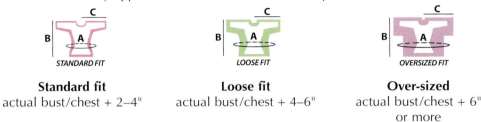

Standard fit	**Loose fit**	**Over-sized**
actual bust/chest + 2–4"	actual bust/chest + 4–6"	actual bust/chest + 6" or more

HOW DO YOU PUT ALL THIS SIZE INFORMATION TOGETHER?

The S (M, L, XL, XXL) sizes in which the patterns are offered appear under the fit icons. Here, and in the pattern instructions and drawings, the smallest size is given first, and the larger sizes follow in order and in parentheses. (If there is only one number given, it applies to all sizes.)

Now look at the fit icon. The measurements of the finished garment appear below the icon. A = chest measurement, B = back length, C = measurement from center back to wrist/lowest point of sleeve.

If you knit to gauge, and you do not SHORTEN OR LENGTHEN, you will achieve these measurements.

WHAT ABOUT HEIGHT?

The garments in this book are made to fit the standard heights of 5'4"-5'6" for a woman or 5'10"–6' for a man. If you are shorter, you will want to make your garment shorter. If you are taller, you will want to make your garment longer. How do you do this? If you are 2" shorter than standard, subtract 1" in length where the pattern says SHORTEN OR LENGTHEN HERE. If you are 4" shorter, subtract 2". If you are 2" taller than standard, add 1" in length wherever the pattern says SHORTEN OR LENGTHEN HERE. If you are 4" taller, add 2".

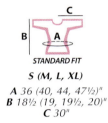

S (M, L, XL)
A 36 (40, 44, 47½)"
B 18½ (19, 19½, 20)"
C 30"

The fact that these garments are made to standard height explains why the back length is pretty much the same for all sizes. If you're 5'4", it doesn't matter if you're an S or an XXL; your shoulders are still the same distance from the floor.

And what about that back neck-to-wrist measurement? Do you remember the Leonardo da Vinci drawing of the man with his arms extended, standing within a square? Da Vinci illustrated that your 'wingspan' is usually the same as your height. So, if you are 5'4", regardless of garment size, you will still measure pretty much the same from your back neck to wrist.

Having said all that, in these patterns you might notice a slight increase in garment length for larger sizes. This is for better overall proportion. You will not see a slight difference in neck to cuff distance, because I do not think it necessary in the looser-fitting, garter stitch garments of this book. However, if your arms are longer than standard, you probably know this and will be prepared to lengthen your sleeves.

Buying yarn

The pattern you choose will suggest a particular quantity of yarn for the size you choose to knit. **This is not necessarily the quantity of yarn you ought to buy.**

HOW MUCH YARN DO YOU BUY?
In the vitals column, you are told a quantity of yarn to buy. For example, for a sweater with five sizes S (M, L, XL XXL), it may read 1000 (1200, 1400, 1600, 1800) yds. You need to translate this information to determine the number of balls you need. Here are the steps to follow.

- First, choose your size; let's say L— the third size.
- Now find the yardage recommended for the third size; in the sample above, L = 1400 yds.
- Look at the label for the yarn you are considering, and find its yardage; let's say it reads 98 yds.
- Divide the yardage you need by the yarn's yardage; in this sample, 1400 ÷ 98 = 14.28. (Use a calculator for this.)
- Round up to the nearest whole number, and this indicates the number of balls you should buy; in this sample, it would be 15.

Is this really and truly the number of balls you need to buy? Perhaps. But what if the result had been 15.05? Would you have bought 15 or 16 balls? And what if you intend to SHORTEN OR LENGTHEN? And what if your row gauge is a little different? And what if our estimates are a little off? (They are only estimates, and we are only human.)

Once you do the math to determine how many balls you need, buy that amount but ask if the yarn shop owner will hold an extra ball or two until you finish. Alternatively, buy an extra ball or two, and ask if you can return what you don't use. (Both are usually possible, within a reasonable period of time.) If it is not possible to hold or return yarn, buy a little extra and realize that what you don't use will be dedicated to your 'yarn stash.' (All truly serious knitters have one!)

As you buy this yarn, be sure it is all of the same dye lot.

WHAT IS A DYE LOT?
A dye lot is a batch of yarn dyed at the same time: the batch is designated by a number, found on the yarn label. Different dye lots in the same color can have slight variations in color, and this will show in the garment. You don't want this. Check all dye lot numbers on all the yarn you wish to buy, to be sure they match.

When we refer to a ball of yarn, this isn't necessarily how it is packaged. Yarn can come in a ball, on a cone, or in a skein. For the first two, nothing need be done—although if you pull the yarn from the center of the ball rather than the outside, you will have less tangling. For the latter, you will need to wind the skein into a ball before working with it—by hanging the skein over the back of a chair, over your knees, or over the hands of someone who loves you.

Yes, you need a calculator for this. The yarn shop will have one, because they do these calculations all the time, But you'll probably want one for when you find wonderful yarn in out-of-the-way places.

Every knitter has failed to check dye lots or been tempted to buy unmatched dye lots. (The latter is usually accompanied by, "It shouldn't matter; I could just work two rows in each dye lot for an inch, and maybe I won't see the switch."). It does matter. Don't buy unmatched dye lots.

Collecting supplies

Besides yarn and needles, there are other standard tools all knitters should carry.

- a flexible tape measure (to measure gauge and your knitting in progress)
- a blunt-tipped tapestry needle (to sew with)
- small scissors (to cut yarn and trim tails)
- stitch holders (to hold live stitches that will be worked later, although a piece of yarn threaded onto a tapestry needle and run through these stitches will work fine)
- markers (to hang on your needle or knitting, designating something that matters; sometimes a paper clip or some yarn will work fine)
- a row counter (if you have days like I do when you can't count to 4!)
- point protectors (to keep your stitches from falling off your needle when you put your knitting down, although a rubber band or elastic hair band wrapped around the end of the needle works)
- a calculator (for when you need to 'do the math')
- a needle gauge (to identify all your unmarked needles)
- non-rusting pins

The other thing you might treat yourself to—once you're truly committed—is a decent knitting bag. So many of us carry our knitting around in grocery bags! What does *that* say about our craft?!

Photocopying your pattern

It is perfectly reasonable to photocopy a pattern you have purchased—along with its abbreviations and special instructions—for your own use. There are things you can do with a photocopy that you might not choose to do with an original: enlarge it, circle the numbers corresponding to the size you are making, write notes in the margins.

Keeping a knitting journal

It's a good idea to keep a record of your knitting experiences. You might address any or all of the following.

- What yarn did you use? (Keep your swatch, and attach the label and a few yards of yarn to it.)
- What needle size did you use to get gauge?
- What size did you make? (Perhaps make a copy of the schematics, noting changes that you made.)
- How many balls did it take?
- How did you launder it?
- Did the measurements change after laundering?
- How much time did it take to finish it?

Knitters actually hate the question, "How long did it take?" But how cool to know the answer!

Knitting is not going to be fun if you make mistakes that you can see but can't fix. And the *making mistakes* part is not the problem. It's the *not fixing them* that ruins the fun.

The techniques in the following chapter will help you fix your mistakes, and not in a way that will make your knitting look cobbled-together. These are the *real deal* solutions that correct, rather than cover up, mistakes. If you use them, your product will be worth the process.

Oops!

And as you master these rescue techniques, something else—something quite wonderful—should begin to happen. You should begin to understand your knitting: its structure, its process. You'll become more intuitive, you'll be able to fix mistakes on your own, you'll find your own ways of doing things.

Of course, sometimes, the only solution is to rip and start over. I admit, freely, that I do this a lot. (Chris will lean over and say, ever so sweetly, "Dear, you're knitting backwards again." Yes, dear, if that's what it takes.)

I once had a knitter hang up on me when I suggested there was no rescue other than to rip. And please believe that I understand how much you don't want to undo—and then redo—your knitting. But there are three things to say in defense of this activity.

1 If it's worth doing, it's worth doing right. (You had to know I was going to say that!)

2 The earlier you discover your mistake, the less ripping—and re-knitting— you'll need to do, so be rigorous in your examination of your work.

3 While you rip, remind yourself that the very next thing you were going to do—once you finished this piece—was to find more knitting. You just found more knitting!

The e-wrap cast-on actually has a bad rep because
• it can drop off the needle too easily,
• it can be loose and sloppy.

Here are solutions to both of these problems. Given how useful it is, and how easily fixed, this cast-on should get more respect!

If an e-wrap cast-on stitch drops off

Sometimes an e-wrap cast-on stitch falls off the needle But here's an easy solution to that problem.

1 As you knit the first row, if one of the cast-on stitches drops off …

2 …put right-hand needle, from back to front, under the slack yarn …

3 …then put left-hand needle through as shown. Wrap the yarn around the right-hand needle, and knit as usual.

4 If more than one stitch falls off, repeat this maneuver with the slack yarn until all the stitches have been recovered.

If you need to tighten an e-wrap cast-on

Despite your best efforts, this cast-on can open up on you. Here's how to make it neater.

1 Begin at the end of the cast-on, where the tail isn't.
With a knitting or tapestry needle, gently pull the first loop towards you.

2 Gently pull the next loop towards you, pulling the excess thread from the previous loop through.

3 As you work along this edge, the excess thread will become longer (above). Just keep pulling it through until you are at the beginning of the cast-on.

4 If you began with a slip knot, you will have to undo this knot (instructions follow) to pull the excess through.

5 To finish, cut tail to desired length.

Getting rid of the slip knot

Some cast-on methods (the crochet, the knitted) need to begin with a slip knot. But there is an ugly knot left by this slip knot that can distort this corner of your work and make seaming awkward. Here's how to remove it.

1 Find it.

2 Remove it.

3 Admire the result!

If you leave your knitting mid-row

Because life has a way of intruding, you really do need to be able to leave your knitting in the middle of a row.

Recognize that your old stitches should be on the left-hand needle, and your new stitches should be on the right-hand needle with the working yarn attached. The piece above is ready to work.

Here the new stitches with the working yarn attached are on the left-hand needle. This piece is 'backwards' and needs to be turned around before working.

My grandmother was a wonderful knitter, and her advice was to "always finish the row," else I would get holes in my knitting.

I still like the discipline of always finishing a row. And it is a great excuse to keep knitting a while longer!

If you drop a stitch/Stitch orientation

Don't panic! This happens all the time! What to do? You want to just put the stitch back onto the left-hand needle, don't you? But there is a right way to do this.

Here is the proper orientation of a stitch.

1 Here's what a dropped stitch looks like (above).

2 Put the dropped stitch back onto your left needle, and look at it before knitting.

3 If it looks like this, it is oriented properly: the side of the stitch nearest you is closer to the tip of the needle than the side of the stitch farthest from you. You may knit this stitch as usual.

4 If it looks like this, it is oriented improperly: the side of the stitch closest to you is farther from the tip of the needle. The stitch looks more open and is on the needle 'backwards.'

5 You may remove it, turn it around, put it back on, then knit as usual. Or ...

6 ... if your stitch is backwards, put your right-hand needle through the far side (the back) of the stitch, and then knit it as usual. Knitting through the back of the stitch will orient it properly.

If you knit through the front of a stitch that is sitting on the needle backwards (see Step 4), you will produce a twisted stitch. (A twisted stitch is not so visible in garter stitch, but it can be very visible in other stitch patterns.)

If a stitch becomes unknit in stockinette stitch

Sometimes we drop a stitch, and it pulls itself loose for one row.

If you have just dropped a stitch, chances are it did not come unknit. Consider your work from both sides. Do you see any loose threads? If not, continue with the steps shown above. If you do see a loose thread, your stitch has come unknit for one row, and you need to work the maneuver shown at right.

1 When just one row has become unknit, you will see only one loose thread on the wrong side of your work.

2 Put the unknit stitch onto the left-hand needle. If you insert the left-hand needle so it is pointing away from you, this will orient the stitch properly.

3 Pick up the loose thread with the right-hand needle ...

If a stitch becomes unknit in garter stitch

Sometimes we drop a stitch, and it pulls itself loose for one row.

1 When only one row has become unknit, you will see only one loose thread, no matter which way you turn your work. Hold your work so the loose thread is on the side of the work facing you.

2 Put right-hand needle through the unknit stitch. If you insert the right-hand needle so it is pointing towards you, this will orient the stitch properly.

3 Put left-hand needle through the stitch so it sits behind right-hand needle.

4 Put right-hand needle under the loose thread.

5 With right-hand needle, pull the loose thread through the stitch.

6 Remove left-hand needle.

7 Put the re-knit stitch onto left-hand needle (photos above). Now treat this re-knit stitch as usual.

4 ...and put it onto the left-hand needle.

5 With the right-hand needle ...

...pass the unknit stitch over the loose thread (above).
6 Now treat this re-knit stitch as usual.

If you need to go back in this row

Sometimes you made a mistake earlier in a row, and you want to fix it. Here's how to unknit back to a mistake.

1 Do not turn your work.

2 Put left-hand needle, pointing away from you, through stitch below first stitch on right-hand needle.

3 Pull the right-hand needle out of its stitch (above). Then pull working yarn free. Repeat Steps 2–3 until you are where you want to be.

If you need to go back many rows/ripping

Sometimes you really do just have to bite the bullet and rip back a number of rows. There may be a dropped stitch that wasn't noticed or a slip stitch that wasn't slipped. It happens to everyone, and ripping is the remedy. And there are a couple of ways to do this . . . ways that make this task a little less terrifying.

One way is to rip back only to the row before where you want to be. Then, as you rip this final row, do so one stitch at a time, putting each new stitch onto a needle as it becomes available. Then before knitting, read Orientation of a stitch (page 146).

Another option, shown below, is particularly easy to do with garter stitch.

1 Find the row to which you want to rip back. Put a needle through . . .

2 . . . the bumps of this row (above). Now rip back, and you'll find your stitches already on a needle. When you knit them, pay attention to their orientation.

3 This option is also available for stockinette stitch. Do just as directed for garter stitch. It is not as easy to stay in the same row of bumps, but you need to do so. When you knit them, pay attention to their orientation.

If you need to tighten a bound-off edge

Sometimes, especially around a neck, the finished edge can be a little loose. The good news is that it can be tightened!

1 Hold work so tail of bind-off is to left. Look at your bind-off. You should see chained loops, moving from right to left. These are what you will tighten, moving from the beginning of the row to the tail.

2 Put needle (knitting or tapestry) under front edge of first loop (above). Pull the thread towards you, then remove the needle.

3 Find the back edge of this same loop (which is quite small, because it was pulled tight by the previous maneuver). Put the needle under it, pull the excess thread through (above), then remove the needle. Put needle under front edge of next loop, pull the excess thread through, then remove the needle.

4 Repeat Steps 3–4 , drawing excess yarn along.

A tightened bind-off

Here are extra tips for tightening the bind-off.

- **If you get stuck along the way, try using your fingers instead of the needle.**
- **If you get really stuck, it could be that you split your yarn during your bind off; you will have to rip out the bind-off and redo it.**
- **Do not over-tighten. If you do, you must remove and re-do your bind-off.**
- **At the end of the row, you might have to undo the last bound-off stitch to draw the excess yarn through.**

If you forgot...

IF YOU FORGOT TO WORK AN INCREASE OR DECREASE

If you have worked past a row in which you were supposed to make an increase or decrease, just make it where it belongs, the next time you are at that spot.

IF YOU MISPLACED A DECREASE

My goodness! Where could it be?

A misplaced decrease would be a knit two together done in the wrong stitches. This might matter. If you look at the crown of a hat, it has lovely pie-shaped wedges because the decreases were worked in the right stitches. If you decrease in the wrong place, your wedge will get messed up. You really should rip back (page 148) to where these stitches were improperly decreased and re-work them. You'll be glad you did!

IF YOU FORGOT TO WORK A YARN OVER

Sometimes a yarn over is just an increase; see above.

But sometimes the yarn over is for a buttonhole and, for the symmetry of your garment, you really want the buttonhole where it was supposed to be. In this case, rip back (page 148), and work the yarn over where directed.

**Decreases align, to form
pie-shaped wedges**

If your knitting has a hole in it

If you dropped a stitch and didn't notice it, you'll have a dropped stitch, a hole, and one less stitch on your needle.

You may rip back to the hole (page 148). But the garter stitch fabric is pretty forgiving, and you might try the following.

   1 Find the dropped stitch.

   2 Secure it by threading a 6" piece of yarn through it.

   3 Sew in tails to wrong side. The result might not be visible on the right side, but you will have one less stitch on your needle than when you started.

SUPPLIERS

Aurora Yarns
Distributes Garnstudio
2385 Carlos St
Moss Beach, CA 94038

Berroco, Inc
PO Box 367
Uxbridge, MA 01569
www.berroco.com

Cascade Yarns
1224 Andove Park E.
Tukwila, WA 98188

Classic Elite Yarns
300 Jackson St.
Lowell, MA 01852

Diamond Yarn
Distributes Sirdar, Noro, and Reynolds in Canada
155 Martin Ross, Unit 3
Toronto, Ontario M3J 2L9 Canada
www.diamondyarn.com

Great Adirondack Yarn Co.
950 Co. Hwy 126
Amsterdam, NY 12010

Knitting Fever Inc
Distributes Noro in USA
35 Debevoise Ave
Roosevelt, NY 11575
www.knittingfever.com

Mission Falls
Distributes Mission Falls in Canada
PO Box 224
Consecon, Ontario K0K IT0 Canada

Mountain Colors Yarn
PO Box 156
Corvallis, MT 59828
www.mountaincolors.com

Muench Yarns Inc
285 Bel Marin Keys Blvd., Unit J
Novato, CA 94949
www.muenchyarns.com

Needful Yarns Inc.
Distributes Lano Gatto
4476 Chesswood Dr. #10,11
Toronto, ON M3J 2B9 Canada
www.needfulyarnsinc.com

Patons Yarns
PO Box 40
Listowel, ON N4W 3H3 Canada
www.patonsyarns.com

Prism
2595 30th Ave N
St. Petersburg, FL 33713

JCA, Inc.
Distributes Reynolds and Istex in US
35 Scales Lane
Townsend, MA 01469-1094

Schaefer Yarn Co LTD
3514 Kelly's Corners Rd
Interlaken, NY 14847

SR Kertzer LTD
Distributes Naturally, Stylecraft and Istex in Canada
105A Winges Road
Woodbridge, ON L4L 6C2 Canada
www.kertzer.com

Swedish Yarn Imports
Distributes Sandnes
PO Box 2069
Jamestown, NC 27282

Tahki/Stacy Charles Inc
8000 Cooper Ave
Bldg 1
Glendale, NY 11385
www.tahkistacycharles.com

Trendsetter
16745 Saticoy St #101
Van Nuys, CA 91406

Unique Kolours LTD
Distributes Mission Falls in US
1428 Oak Lane
Dowingtown, PA 19335
www.uniquekolours.com

YARN WEIGHTS

	Super fine	Fine	Light	Medium	Bulky	Super Bulky
Numbering System	1	2	3	4	5	6
Yarn Weight Category	Super fine	Fine	Light	Medium	Bulky	Super Bulky
Also called	Sock Fingering Baby	Sport Baby	DK Light Worsted	Worsted Afghan	Chunky Craft Aran	Bulky Roving Rug
Knit Gauge Range in Stockinette Stitch to 10cm/4 inches	27 to 32 sts	23 to 26 sts	21 to 24 sts	16 to 20 sts	12 to 15 sts	6 to 11 sts
Recommended Needle (metric)	2mm to 3.25mm	3.25 to 3.75mm	3.75mm to 4.50mm	4.5mm to 5.5mm	5.5mm to 8mm	9mm to 16mm
Recommended Needle (US)	1 to 3	3 to 5	5 to 7	7 to 9	9 to 11	13 to 19

Every pattern in this book tells you what weight yarn to use. To find an appropriate yarn, look at the name by which it is also called (above), then look at your pattern for the gauge over 10cm/4", and the needle size used. Look on the label of the yarn you are considering for matching information.

B   **Back** The part of the garment worn to the back of the body or the side of the knitting not facing while working a row or round

beginning with What you will do next

binding off Closing off stitches

blocking A finishing procedure to which you submit your pieces

casting on Creating a number of stitches, usually by adding them onto the left-hand needle

cm   **centimeter** Measure of length equaling .4 of 1"

decreasing Removing a stitch by making two stitches into one

dpn(s)   **double-pointed needle(s)** Needles with points at both ends

ending with What you have just finished doing

F   **Front** The part of the garment worn to the front of the body or the side of the knitting facing while working a row or round

garter stitch The fabric produced by knitting all stitches, all rows

increasing Adding a stitch by making one stitch into two

k   **knit** Produce a knit stich

kb   **knit into the back of a stitch** Knit into the part of the stitch on the back of the needle

kf   **knit into the front of a stitch** Knit into the part of the stitch on the front of the needle

kf&b   **knit into the front and back of a stitch** Knit into the front and then the back of the same stitch

knit stitch A stitch with its 'bump' to the back

k-wise   **knit-wise** As if to knit

L   **Left (Front or Back)** The part of the garment worn on the left of the body

live stitches Stitches left behind, by turning before the end of a row

M1   **Make 1** Increase by picking up the thread between the needles and knitting into the back of it

picking up Forming stitches by inserting left-hand needle, from left to right, along a finished edge, without using yarn and without knitting a new row

picking up and knitting Forming stitches by moving from right to left, inserting right-hand needle into a finished edge, using yarn and knitting a new row

p   **purl stitch** A stitch with its 'bump' to the front (not something we show you how to produce in this book)

p-wise   **purl-wise** As if to purl

rev St st   **reverse stockinette stitch** The bumpy side of the fabric that is produced by knitting all stitches in rounds or by purling all stitches on wrong-side rows and knitting all stitches on right-side rows when working flat

ridge The horizontal line of bumps produced by knitting 2 rows (working garter stitch)

R   **Right (Front or Back)** The part of the garment worn on the right of the body

RS   **right side(s)** The 'public' side(s) of the garment

rnd   **round** A row worked circularly, with no turning at the end

row A row worked flat, turning at the end

short row A row with stitches left behind, by turning before the end of a row

sl   **slip** Transfer a stitch from left- to right-hand needle without working it

SKP   **slip one, knit 1, pass slip stitch over** Slip first stitch from left-hand needle knit-wise, knit the next stitch on left-hand needle, then pass the slip stitch over the stitch just knit

sl 1 k-wise   **slip one knit-wise** Slip the next stitch on the left-hand needle, as if to knit

sl 1 p-wise   **slip one purl-wise** Slip the next stitch on the left-hand needle, as if to purl

sl st   **slip stitch** A stitch formed by transferring it from left-hand needle to right-hand needle without working it

st(s)   **stitch(es)** Loop(s) formed with yarn on the knitting needles

St st   **stockinette stitch** The smooth side of the fabric that is produced by knitting all stitches in rounds or by knitting all stitches on right-side rows and purling all stitches on wrong-side rows when working flat

tail The 'thread' left hanging at the beginning or end of a ball or piece

turn Turn work to opposite side, even if in the middle of a row

yb	**with yarn in back** With working yarn on the side of your knitting not facing you		**working straight** Continuing without any shaping (increasing, decreasing, etc.)
yf	**with yarn in front** With working yarn on the side of your knitting facing you	**WS**	**Wrong side(s)** The 'non-public' side(s) of the garment
	working flat Working a row, turning the piece, then working the next row	**yd**	**yard** Measure of length equaling 36" or .9144 meter (m)
			yarn The 'thread' with which you will form stitches
	working in rounds Working a row, then working the next row without turning the piece (also known as *working circularly*)	**yo**	**yarn over** A stitch produced by simply laying yarn over the right-hand needle

Table of comparative ratios

For this book—when seaming the sleeves into armholes for Sally's Favorite Summer Sweater—use this table as follows:

- divide the number of sts (the smaller number) by the number of R's (garter ridges, the larger number);
- find the closest fraction;
- seam as directed.

The fraction	*What it means*	*How to seam*
.5 = 1/2	1st / 2R's	Seam 1st to 2R's
.6 = 3/5	3sts / 5R's	(Seam 1st to 2 R's) twice, then seam 1st to 1R once
.6667 = 2/3	2sts / 3R's	Seam 1st to 2R's, then seam 1st to 1R
.714 = 5/7	5sts / 7R's	(Seam 1 st to 2R's) twice, then (seam 1st to 1R) three times
.75 = 3/4	3sts / 4R's	(Seam 1st to 1R) twice, then seam 1st to 2R's once
.8 = 4/5	4sts / 5R's	(Seam 1st to 1R) 3 times, then seam 1st to 2R's once
.85 = 6/7	6sts / 7R's	(Seam 1st to 1R) 5 times, then seam 1st to 2R's once
.9 = 9/10	9sts / 10R's	(Seam 1st to 1R) 8 times, then seam 1st to 2R's once

To convert inches measurement to centimeters

Simply multiply the inches by 2.5 For example: 4" x 2.5 = 10cm

This table is useful whenever you are seaming stitches into rows and you are facing something other than a 1-to-1 ratio. Here's how it works:
- **if using this table in a garter stitch garment, R = a garter ridge (2 rows of knitting);**
- **for other stitch patterns, R might = a row (1 row of knitting);**
- **with very few exceptions, the number of sts will be smaller than the the number of R's, so just use the table as directed.**

PROJECT INDEX

MEDITATION INDEX

ACKNOWLEDGEMENTS

This book is dedicated to all those of generous heart and patient hands who have taught someone to knit, especially my mother, Dodie Melville.

The material of this book comes from three sources:
1. what I sorted out on my own (not that I presume to be the only one to have made these discoveries);
2. what I learned from others and have adapted (not that I am the only one to have made these adaptations);
3. what I learned from others that is part of knitting's common lexicon.

I am entirely grateful to every teacher and every knitting book from whence I have learned.

Thanks to the amazing production team at XRX: Alexis (for his humor and gorgeous photos, both of which we have come to expect), Bob (for his gentle sensibility), David (for his attention to detail and ability to do whatever asked), Elaine (for making some of the best decisions of this book plus just being a good friend), Jay (for being so very responsive plus knowing how to knit), Natalie (for her patience and dedication), Rick (for his graciousness in the face of my demands), plus Carol, Denny, Ev, Holly, Jason, Karen, and Sue.

Thanks to Gail McHugh, Jean Parker, Tricia Siemens, and Beverley Slopen for their enthusiasm and advice.

Thanks to the knitters who produced or test knit some of the pieces in this book: Aggie Beynon, Mel Biggs, Heather Daymond, Barbara Hull, Caddy Ledbetter, (I wish I could add Jeremy Ledbetter; perhaps the next book?), Beth Merikle, Lynn Philips, Laurel Thom, Jen Woolner, and—above all—Stasia Bania (without whom I could not function).

Thanks to the yarn companies and shop owners who helped out, especially Bev Nimon, Josie Dolan, the two Julias, Julie Schilthuis (of the Needle Emporium), plus Carol and Ron (of The Mannings).

Finally, thanks to Chris Hatton . . . who is more wonderful than I could have imagined and more patient than I deserve.

ALEXIS XENAKIS

COLOPHON:

~~ONLIGHT~~ KNITTING IN THE MOONLIGHT ~~KNITTIN~~

Lake Ontario stretches out in front of us, not yet bathed in the soft reds of sunrise. It's early morning near the Sky Dome in Toronto, and we should be working, but we've dropped anchor at a Harbourfront Starbuck's.

Shortly, our Canada shoot for Sally Melville's *The Knitting Experience* will be in full swing. For the moment, on this unseasonably cold June morning, we're warmed by lattés and the glorious sunrise. But it's time to let the locals know we're here.

"Homer! Homer! Homer!" On cue, Sally Melville's schnauzer comes running on deck of the *Mon Ark*, barking back a welcome. Sally and her husband, entrepreneur Chris Hatton, are also on deck, sipping their morning brew and waving hello.

The caffeine jolt provides that extra kick needed to clamber up the boat. The *Mon Ark*, Captain Chris proudly tells us, is "an ocean-going, steel-hulled, 43-foot cruiser, with a 60-foot mast. I climb it regularly." The *Mon Ark*'s interior is appointed in warm, white ash ("a real Canadian wood") and

that makes for a warm galley. "Like being in a cottage," says the captain. "Close the hatch when it's snowing, fire the small furnace, and it's a very warm, small, cozy space."

Sailing, in the snow? "It's just like sailing in the rain," he continues. "I used to live on the boat all winter long, and people said to me, 'Isn't it cold in the winter time?' But Sally and I are not warm-weather people; we love being out in the cold. Living on a boat in Canada, it never gets warm. In the middle of the hottest day of the summer, out on the water, it might get up to 70 degrees."

Perfect sweater weather. And speaking of sweaters, what is it like being on board with one of the knitting universe's most prolific knitters?

Two cities on the water, Toronto and the Windy City, provide the backdrop for *The Knitting Experience*—(Counterclockwise, from left) A Chicago iron lace landmark and the XRX crew headed by Fashion Editor Rick Mondragon; Captain Chris Hatton and Sally Melville harborside; visitors on our Toronto set; the *Mon Ark* with an additional sail, a photographer's silk; one of Sally's few non-knitting moments with Homer; Buckingham Fountain lights up our Chicago set; Sally and Homer on guard in downtown Toronto; sails unfurl on Lake Ontario; our Canada crew hams it up with a northern tourist.

THE MOONLIGHT KNITTING IN THE MOONLIGHT

"Sally knits all day, everywhere. It's incessant. Knitting is what she does when the rest of us are breathing. She cannot sit, watch television, or read a book without knitting. She eats without knitting, but the knitting is right beside her waiting for the last bite.

"Being on the water is so peaceful, restful, relaxing. Sally will be knitting on deck, the sun will be setting. I get to do my thing and she gets to do her thing. She lives as much for her knitting as I live for my sailing."

Okay, we all know about the peace. What about the 'Eureka!' moments? "Ninety per cent of Sally's 'Eureka!' moments happen in the middle of the night," Chris says. "She'll wake up at three o'clock in the morning and start scribbling down notes for

a solution that came to her. I love watching the creative process: if you look at Sally and what surrounds her, it's all about bringing two different things together. Sally's son, Jeremy, mixes soul and calypso into a different genre. Her daughter, Caddy, combines two diverse cooking traditions to create fabulous culinary sensations."

Our floating headquarters, moored in the Harbourfront Marina, is another example of the dualities in Sally's life: *Mon Ark*, stands for both 'My Ark' and the beautiful butterflies that decorate its stern.

It's time for Chris to trade his captain's hat for that of a photo assistant—he's volunteered to hold the silk that will diffuse the sun's rays, and keep the garment colors vivid. During a lull in the shoot, while Photo Stylist Bev Nimon preps a model, Chris is joined by our volunteer assistants, the two Julias (Granau and Dinner), and Toronto's famous son, the pianist Glenn Gould, in bronze. We're outside the renowned pianist's old studio, adding our shoot to the busy pace that is downtown Toronto. "This is fun," Chris says. "This really *is* the birth of the book, isn't it?"

"What was it like watching that shoot?" Sally asks. "Suddenly my work was in other people's hands. It was exciting to see the book come to life, but a bit scary. That was my baby walking out the door." Sally, in an airport limo, is heading from Stitches Midwest to O'Hare for a flight back home to Canada. She taught a full schedule at Stitches, then

an intensive Stitches Etc. workshop. Yet, like the professional she is, she patiently fields more questions.

"Knitting on the boat? It's magic. When you travel on the water you don't see the land the same way; it's a very different perspective on your country and environment. The pace slows down—you can walk somewhere almost as fast as you can sail there. You are at the mercy of nature—so you live a different life; you just have to go with the flow."

Did Sally just utter her knitting mantra?

She laughs. "I guess. You know I do these talks on creativity. The first stage in the creative process is to establish a problem that needs to be solved. The world's most creative people say that their best work comes at a point of interface between subject, culture, discipline, and technique. It's as simple as putting two contradictory ideas together, and it's as complex as intersecting Guatemalan weaving with Fair Isle technique.

"Creativity happens when you bump things together, connect the unconnected, see relationships others don't see. When you have a lot of things going on in your life—different interests,

you travel, you try new techniques, you expose yourself to different cultures and disciplines— you've got more of these points of intersection."

It all sounds great, but rather serious. And this book looks like so much fun…

Sally, being the great teacher—and seafarer—she is, takes a different tack: "Creativity challenges basic assumptions. Look at the cover sweater: none of the bottom edges match. The reason for that is this: beginners *can* knit a sweater side-to-side; they cast on for the left front, cast on for the back, and cast on for the right front.

"And with this sweater it doesn't matter if they don't cast on the right number of stitches! If they get it wrong, let's just get it wrong *deliberately*. If nothing matches, there's no such thing as a mistake! The only thing they have to do is make their sleeves the same length—and I help them figure out how to do that."

You almost think you hear the class bell ringing as Sally sums it up. But it's only interference on the cell phone: "The creative intersection in *The Knitting Experience* is this: I want beginners to be

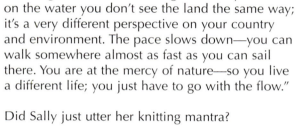

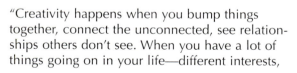

(This page, counterclockwise, from right) Perched at the Palisades; Sally teaching on the shoot; a day for cocoa, not ice cream; our Canada crew celebrates the end of the shoot at Toronto's Sunnyside Bathing Pavilion; a working title for a book on Sally's blackboard; quiet room at the author's condo; Sally and Editor Elaine Rowley at work; staying dry during a Toronto drizzle.

able to knit great, easy stuff that they really want to wear. We usually think that is contradictory. When you're knitting, you get into this wonderful frame of mind where you *are* going with the flow. I want *The Knitting Experience* to be simple enough but attractive enough that everybody will want to get into that state of mind. A place where you have no sense of time, where life feels quite magical."

Like sailing and knitting under a full moon.

But Sally didn't spend *all* her time on the Great Lakes. One chilly spring morning she found herself strapped to a harness, dangling from the rock face of the Palisades State Park near Sioux Falls. What else was a photographer to do in coming up with cover possibilities for a book whose working title was *The Knitting Revolution*?

"*Knitting Revolution*, indeed," Sally says. "Strap you up in a harness and hang you from the Palisades! Someone who's terrified of heights! I hear, normally, authors aren't allowed on photo shoots, let alone strung up on one!"

Only a foot or so separated Sally from the chasm—and the churning water, a hundred feet

below. Were we in danger of losing our fearless knitter? Rapelling ropes anchored Sally to the rock and then wrapped around the body of our friendly rock-climbing guide, Gary Johnson, who was happy to join our chilly Palisades climb.

"I fell in love with a simple aesthetic," Sally says as her cell phone signal fades. "Very simple, very wearable, very classic garments. It's an elegant aesthetic that doesn't go out of style, that appeals to everyone. I want everyone to share in *The Knitting Experience*, everyone to come along for the journey."

I can't wait to take you behind the scenes of our next adventure.

—Alexis Xenakis
Sioux Falls, South Dakota

(This page, counterclockwise, from right) All tangled up during a shoot; sharing a moment with the captain; Styling Intern Hannah Sorenson wrapped up in her job; our author-turned-model and Mayor Gary Hanson at Sioux Falls City Hall; all-terrain knitter; Julia Granau, Captain Chris, and Julia Dinner with Glenn Gould outside the master's studio; Editor Elaine Rowley (second from right) stepping up a notch on the corporate ladder; Photo Stylist Bev Nimon unwinding—it was a memorable knitting experience for all of us.

also from XRX Books

Gerdine Strong
ANGELS: A KNITTER'S DOZEN

Susan Mills & Norah Gaughan
THE BEST OF LOPI

Priscilla A. Gibson-Roberts
ETHNIC SOCKS & STOCKINGS

Meg Swansen
A GATHERING OF LACE

Cheryl Potter
HANDPAINT COUNTRY

·KIDS·KIDS·KIDS·

Anna Zilboorg
MAGNIFICENT MITTENS

Jean Moss
SCULPTURED KNITS

The Best of Knitter's
SHAWLS AND SCARVES

·SOCKS·SOCKS·SOCKS·

Sally Melville
STYLES

The Best of Weaver's
FABRICS THAT GO BUMP

The Best of Weaver's
HUCK LACE

The Best of Weaver's
THICK 'N THIN

KNITTER'S Magazine

visit us online at
www.knittinguniverse.com

Join the knitters' support
network: KnitU listserve at
www.knittinguniverse.com

All photography by Alexis Xenakis